W9-AGD-098

ABOUT THE AUTHOR

Kathy Flanigan is a reporter for the *Milwaukee Journal Sentinel* and for TapMilwaukee.com for which she covers the region's craft-beer community. She lives in Milwaukee.

BEER LOVER'S WISCONSIN

KATHY FLANIGAN

Globe Pequot
Guilford, Connecticut

my husband, Jim,
elop an even greater
appreciation and passion for all things beer. 

Globe Pequot

An imprint of Rowman & Littlefield
Distributed by NATIONAL BOOK NETWORK

British Library Cataloguing in Publication Information Available
Library of Congress Cataloging-in-Publication Data Available

ISBN 978-1-4930-2793-4 (paperback)
ISBN 978-1-4930-2794-1 (e-book)

∞™ The paper used in this publication meets the minimum requirements of American National Standard for Information Sciences—Permanence of Paper for Printed Library Materials, ANSI/NISO Z39.48-1992.

ACKNOWLEDGMENTS

I have so many people to thank.

Thank you, Duane Dudek, for being my biggest supporter and my designated driver.

Thank you, Caitlin Cave, for being my cheerleader and my favorite copy editor.

Thank you, Thomas Ciula, for being my beer mentor and having more confidence in my tasting abilities than I do.

Thank you, Lucy Saunders, for recommending me as the potential author of this book.

Thank you, beer community, for being gracious.

Thank you, friends and colleagues for listening to me talk about nothing but this book for months.

Thank you, sisters Peggy, Deb, and Molly, for joining me on a couple of the road trips, and for listening to me talk about nothing but this book for months.

Thank you, Jack, for your constant company.

CONTENTS

INTRODUCTION

Wisconsin, you're pretty.

It's easy to dismiss the state as being only as great as Milwaukee, its largest city, but that discounts its other attributes—clean air, nearly 500,000 acres of state forests, and 15,074 lakes.

Once you look at Wisconsin in its entirety, once you drive it, you recognize that there's more going on here than expected. Lake Michigan hugs the eastern coastline. Lake Superior laps at the shores of its most northern border. A road trip along the western edge of the state follows the Mississippi all the way to Iowa.

In between are miles of verdant farmland dotted with big and small communities. The differences are sometimes stark. No one would confuse Milwaukee with, say, Monroe. But they have one thing in common—beer.

I've lived in this state for twenty-three years and the journey to its more than 150 breweries (give or take a few) still surprised me. The adventure launched at the tip of Wisconsin where the lupine is as colorful as the residents and streets are marked with picket-fence arrows instead of road signs.

The first night's meal—set al fresco—was the result of a tip from another brewery visitor. Freehands Farm isn't the kind of place a newcomer would know about on his own. And it took a handful of phone calls to find it through street construction. The payoff of fine dining in a bucolic setting was the perfect end to a day of exploration.

There were moments in my beer travels that made me laugh out loud—the woman in a fedora singing Frank Sinatra tunes into a karaoke machine and the search for a brewery on a hidden golf course that circled into an apartment complex where the only option was to wave to the stranger sunbathing in a lawn chair. There were a few impromptu, behind-the-scenes tours of breweries so small they used closets with air conditioners as walk-in coolers. There was a generous plate of sausages and crackers at one small brewery and camera lessons from a patron at another. I was invited to watch a hop harvest in progress. There were long rides on lonely highways where I had to pull out an old-school map because my phone didn't get a signal.

There was a stop at the American Legion in Viroqua, a town small enough that you can walk from one end to the other, because someone said they had a grand selection of craft beer. He was right.

Brewers support each other. There was Dave Anderson, owner of Dave's BrewFarm, enjoying a beer at a brewery in LaCrosse. And another time there was Eric Rykal, former brewer at Projekt Brewing in Eau Claire, having a beer at Dave's BrewFarm.

In Milwaukee there was a potluck feast and dog birthday party before a Badgers game at one new brewery, and children running until they were sweaty during a soft opening of another.

While Milwaukee brought the state into craft beer in the 1980s, Madison turned it into a movement, stockpiling craft breweries like squirrels saving for winter. Thank you, Tim Allen, for encouraging so many students in your Plant and Man class at the University of Wisconsin to become brewers.

In other cities, beer found its modern footing with heavy expectations. Villages like Potosi use it as a lifeline to revitalization. Is it working? The new brewery there says yes.

Wisconsin's breweries reflect the state. Macro-brewer MillerCoors leads the way in production but nanobreweries like One Barrel in Madison or any of the state's brewpubs (a legal designation in Wisconsin) have their loyal audiences.

Beer is Wisconsin's heritage. German settlers carried recipes from home and duplicated them by taking advantage of plentiful water sources, fertile soil, and underground caves that mimicked refrigeration.

For a beer-hungry state like Wisconsin, Prohibition hit deep in brewery pockets. Brewers did their best to find ways to make cash despite Prohibition. Frederick Pabst owned 1,500 acres of farmland outside Milwaukee where he raised dairy cows and champion Percheron and Hackney horses. It should come as no surprise then that during Prohibition, the brewery turned to cheese as its main commodity. Among the products was "Pabst-ett" cheese, a precursor to Velveeta, which was sold to Kraft in 1933 at the end of Prohibition, according to *Forbes* magazine.

Pabst, along with Schlitz and Miller also sold malt extract, essentially a kit for making beer at home. Instructions were included.

LAKE SUPERIOR
MINNESOTA
DULUTH
SUPERIOR
APOSTLE ISLANDS
WASHBURN
ASHLAND
IRONWOOD
MARQUETTE
MICHIGAN
CHEQUAMEGON NATIONAL FOREST
DANBURY
HAYWARD
PARK FALLS
LAND O' LAKES
EAGLE RIVER
NICOLET NATIONAL FOREST
SPOONER
PHILLIPS
RHINELANDER
KINSFORD
GREEN BAY
ST. CROIX FALLS
CAMERON
LADYSMITH
MERRILL
NEW RICHMOND
MEDFORD
ANTIGO
MARINETTE
SISTER BAY
EGG HARBOR
DOOR PENINSULA
WISCONSIN
CHIPPEWA FALLS
OCONTO FALLS
PRESCOTT
MENOMONIE
EAU CLAIRE
SHAWANO
STURGEON BAY
MARSHFIELD
CLINTONVILLE
MONDOVI
NEILLSVILLE
STEVENS POINT
GREEN BAY
WHITEHALL
WISCONSIN RAPIDS
WAUPACA
APPLETON
MISSISSIPPI RIVER
BLACK RIVER FALLS
PETENWELL DAM
MANITOWOC
WAUTOMA
CHILTON
TOMAH
CASTLE ROCK LAKE
OSHKOSH
LAKE WINNEBAGO
LA CROSSE
NEW LISBON
SHEBOYGAN
WESTBY
PORTAGE
BEAVER DAM
WEST BEND
LAKE MICHIGA
RICHLAND CENTER
MENOMONEE FALLS
IOWA
BOSCOBEL
LAKE MENDOTA
MADISON
MILWAUKEE
DODGEVILLE
STOUGHTON
LANCASTER
RACINE
JANESVILLE
MONROE
KENOSHA
DUBUQUE
ILLINOIS

Other brewers switched to making soda. The Schlitz family gambled on sweets as an alternative and created the Eline Milk Chocolate bar. One report says the venture lost $17 million.

Archives at the Wisconsin Historical Society maintain that the state's voters were among the first to taper off Prohibition. Voters approved a referendum amending the Volstead Act that allowed for the manufacture and sale of beer with low alcohol. The end of Prohibition is sometimes credited to Wisconsin senator John J. Blaine who proposed a constitutional amendment for its repeal.

The state has always been proud of its brew. Miller Park, home of the Milwaukee Brewers, is named for a brewery. Pabst Theater, draped in baroque and modeled after European opera houses, was commissioned by a beer baron. The sitcom "Laverne & Shirley" was set in a Milwaukee brewery. Four of the oldest operating breweries in America are in Wisconsin—Leinenkugel opened in Chippewa Falls in 1867, Stevens Point Brewery opened in Stevens Point in 1857, Miller Brewing was founded in Milwaukee in 1855, and Minhas started out in Monroe in 1845. Actually, five of the ten oldest breweries are here if you count Pabst, which opened in Milwaukee in 1844 and, so many years later, has settled its innovation brewery at the edge of the original campus where Captain Frederick Pabst ruled.

Beer is such a BIG part of Wisconsin's ethos. The beverage that made Milwaukee famous courses through small towns and mid-size cities alike. In cities like Potosi, the town has pinned its hopes and financial future on the brewery. In Plymouth, the residents treat the brewery as though they're the owners.

New Glarus named its brewery for the town. In return, every bar and restaurant down the hill carries the hometown brew as a badge of pride.

The men and women reviving the craft of brewing beer want to do more than replicate the past. They want to make better beer and they want to share it with you.

The research is over but the adventure hardly ends. New breweries continue to open at a rapid pace. Keeping up is a challenge. And a goal.

I encourage you to take this book along on a trip through Wisconsin. Slow down and take in the state. Stop and eat the cheese curds. Drink the beer. Enjoy.

HOW TO USE THIS GUIDE

This book is organized by region, with breweries listed alphabetically. Where possible I have also provided listings for beer bars, beer-related restaurants, and beer gardens. Each entry provides a brief idea of what to expect at those establishments. I've included addresses, phone numbers, and hours for all. If there's a style that the brewer hangs his or her hat on, I've included it. If there is a beer that really stands out to me, I included a Beer Lover's Pick with tasting notes. I've also included information on tours; where you don't see tour times, you can assume the brewery or brewpub is either too small to accommodate tours or the brewhouse is readily visible from the taproom.

Don't have a favorite beer? Visit a beer bar to sample a variety. Wisconsin has always been known for its neighborhood taverns and watering holes. Let's just say craft beer raised the bar on all of them. For those who appreciate good beer served by a knowledgeable server from clean beer lines and served in a proper glass, consider our picks the best of those places. A shot-and-a-beer place is what you need sometimes.

For those who like to work off their calories, where I could, I've noted bike trails. For the dog lovers among us, I've included places that welcome dogs, and not just on the patio—when I could, I included breweries with dogs on premise.

In addition to these individual entries, you'll also find sections on:

Beer Festivals: Beer loves a party, and they're not just for summer, either. The list of annual beer events includes enough festival opportunities to sample beers to fill a calendar.

Beer Bus Tours, Bike Tours, and More: I've included popular beer tours in Milwaukee and Madison. You'll find information on mobile bars in both those cities. Other cities have approved similar businesses, so expect more to open. This section also has information on Milwaukee's beer history. Visitors can tour the Pabst Mansion, see a performance at the Pabst Theater, and eat lunch at The Brown Bottle, once the taproom for the Schlitz Brewery.

Home Brew Shops: Brewers have to start somewhere. You'll find a list of the home brew shops throughout the state.

In the Kitchen: A few breweries shared popular recipes that use beer. They would love it if you used their beer, but it's possible to substitute a brew in the same style.

This has been my journey. I'm thrilled to share it. But don't be afraid to ask suggestions from the bartender, the brewery or fellow brewery patrons. I've found that many of them are happy to share tips about the beers or food in their city.

GLOSSARY OF TERMS

ABV: Stands for "alcohol by volume" and indicates the percentage of alcohol in a beer. A typical domestic beer is a little less than 5 percent ABV.

Ale: Beer brewed with top-fermenting yeast. Ales are brewed more quickly than yeast beers, which take at least six weeks at cold temperatures. Ambers, stouts, and porters are considered ales.

Altbier: A German style of ale that is usually brown in color with a strong malt backbone.

Barleywine: A beer style with a high ABV. American barleywines are typically made with several hops.

Barrel of beer: Beer production is measured in barrels. A barrel of beer equals 31 gallons.

Beer: An alcoholic beverage brewed with malt, water, hops, and yeast.

Beer bar: A bar with a strong inventory of craft and imported beers and a knowledgeable staff.

Bitter: An English-style ale that is hoppier tasting than an English mild, but less hoppy than an IPA.

Bock: A German style of lager with more malt than hops.

Bomber: A 22-ounce bottle of beer, typically specialty beers or beers from nano-breweries.

Brewpub: In Wisconsin, brewpubs are allowed to produce up to 10,000 barrels of beer per year, as opposed to breweries, which are allowed to produce an unlimited amount of beer.

Cask ales: Naturally carbonated ales poured with a hand pump instead of being forced out with carbon dioxide or nitrogen. Also known as "real ales."

Clone recipe: A home-brew recipe based on a commercial beer.

Contract brewery: A brewery that does not make its beer in house but has it brewed and bottled at another location.

Craft brewery: Independent craft brewers are defined by the Brewers Association as those where less than 25 percent (or equivalent economic interest) of the craft brewery is owned or controlled by an alcohol industry member that is not itself a craft brewer.

Craft brew: The Brewers Association says craft beer is generally made with traditional ingredients such as malted barley with interesting and sometimes non-traditional ingredients often added for distinctiveness.

Crowler: A 32-ounce can of beer typically filled at the brewery or brewpub where it can be sealed by a special machine. Oskar Blues Brewing helped create crowlers, which are thought to last longer because UV rays can't get through the can.

Double: This is sometimes called "imperial" but almost always means a higher alcohol version of a beer. It can also refer to an American version of a Belgian dubbel.

ESB: Extra Special Bitter, a traditional malt-heavy English pub ale with low bitterness.

Gastropub: A beer-centric bar or pub with an emphasis on food. Hinterland in Green Bay is one example.

Gose: A style of beer with a sour wheat flavor with roots in Germany.

Growler: A 64-ounce jug of beer. Milwaukee residents are taught that a growler originated with children who fetched pails of beer (growlers) for workers before Prohibition.

Hops: *Humulus lupulus* is a flower used for flavor and stability in beer.

IBU: International bittering units, used to measure how bitter hops make a beer.

Imperial: A higher-alcohol version of a regular strength beer.

IPA: India pale ale. Thought to be created when the British wanted to take beer to India and used hops to keep it fresh.

Kolsch: Brewed mainly with Pilsner malt, a kolsch is a light ale invented in Germany.

Lager: Beer brewed with bottom-fermenting yeast, a more difficult operation for most brewers, requiring more space and time to ferment and brew.

Malt: Germinated cereal grains that provide the fermentable sugar in beers. The more fermentable sugar, the higher the ABV. Without the malt, a beer would be too bitter from the hops.

Mash: The process of steeping hot water and grains to activate malt enzymes. This converts the starches from the grains into fermentable sugars.

Microbrewery: A small brewery that sells its beer, usually under 15,000 barrels, mostly locally.

Nanobrewery: Typically produces 3 barrels or under in one batch.

Nitro draft: Beers served on draft using kegs pressurized with nitrogen instead of the more common carbon dioxide. This helps create a creamier body, particularly useful with stouts. Some beers can be nitro in bottles or cans.

Pilsner: A style of German or Czech lager, usually light in color.

Porter: A dark ale made with a heavy hand of malts.

Quad: A strong Belgian-style ale, typically sweet and high in alcohol.

Regional brewery: A brewery typically making between 15,000 and 6 million barrels of beer.

Russian imperial stout: A higher alcohol version of a regular stout.

Saison: A French farmhouse ale that is fruity or spicy and often bottle conditioned as it was when French farmers made it.

Seasonal beers: Beer brewed at specific times of the year. For example, an Oktoberfest.

Session beer: A low-alcohol beer, sometimes called a lawn mower beer, one you can have several of in one long "session" of drinking.

Stout: A dark beer brewed with roasted malts.

Strong ale: A style of ale in which alcohol content can reach 12 ABV or higher. Strong ales, like most high ABV beers, can be cellared.

Tap takeover: An event where a bar or pub hosts a brewery and has several of its beers on tap.

Tripel: A Belgian-style malty beer with some spice, first used as a designation by Belgian trappist brewers. A tripel is typically lighter in color than a dubbel but higher in alcohol.

Wheat beer: Top-fermenting beers brewed using wheat along with barley malts. Hefeweizens and witbiers are examples. Lambics, Berlinerweiss, and goses can also be wheat beers.

Wort: The sweet liquid extracted from mixing mash, which is hot water and malts.

Yeast: The living organism in beer that causes the sugars to ferment and become alcohol.

Milwaukee

To understand the resurgence of the craft in the city synonymous with beer is to know how it all began.

Milwaukee's beer story begins at Forest Home Cemetery, the final resting place of four of the city's founding father beer makers. Jacob Best, who founded what would become Pabst Brewing; August Krug, who established the brewery that became known as Schlitz; and Valentin Blatz, who incorporated the Valentin Blatz Brewing Company and produced the first individually bottled beer, are buried there. So is Frederick Pabst, who took over from his father-in-law, Jacob Best.

Some people believe if it weren't for the Chicago Fire in 1871, Milwaukee may have remained a sleepy brewery secret. After the fire, Milwaukee sent barrel after barrel of beer south. Sales of Schlitz beer soared and Schlitz became "the beer that made Milwaukee famous."

There are reminders of that beer heritage everywhere. MillerCoors still brews from the original spot where Frederick Miller founded the brewery in 1855. National League Baseball's Milwaukee Brewers play at Miller Park. It's the city of summer beer gardens and gemutlichkeit. Breweries spread across town, each claiming its own personality.

The city's breweries have the goal they've always had: to brew tasty beer for thirsty people.

Beer is Milwaukee's past and its future. Take a look at it in the present.

1840 BREWING CO.

342 E. Ward St., Milwaukee, WI 53207;
Owners: Stephanie Vetter and Kyle Vetter

Kyle Vetter once worked as the oak manager at Ska Brewing in Aspen, Colorado, but he came back to Milwaukee, where he grew up, to start a business here with his wife Stephanie. A consultant with the Crafter Space brewery incubator program, Vetter runs 1840 Brewing Co., which he describes as an urban warehouse. The name 1840 refers to the first year commercial brewing started in Milwaukee. 1840 Brewing will open to the public in July 2017.

He purchases wort from other brewers and then creates barrel-aged beers using Old World techniques. The beers age three months to three years. He opens the taproom once a month and has four to ten beers on tap at a time. Visitors are invited to bring in their own food. He recently started a Members Club in which people sign up to receive one release a month.

THE BAVARIAN BIERHAUS

700 W. Lexington Blvd., Glendale, WI 53217; (414) 316-9583;
thebavarianbierhaus.com

Founded: 2016 **Founders:** Mike Weiss and management team Scott Elsaesser and Laura Krauser **Brewers:** Nate Bahr (brewmaster) and Mike Biddick **Flagship beers:** Helles, Hefeweizen, Drunkel, and Zwickel **Seasonal beers:** Oktoberfest, Christmas bock, and Maibock **Tours:** By request **Taproom hours:** Sun, 11 a.m. to 9 p.m.; Tues through Thurs, noon to 10 p.m.; and Fri through Sat, noon to midnight

German lagers are the mainstay at The Bavarian Bierhaus, which is, as it should be, in a German-style restaurant and brewery where the waitstaff wear dirndls and lederhosen even when it's not Oktoberfest season.

In trying to stay true to style, Nick Bahr and Mike Biddick created a rye IPA recipe that they turned into a lager. They also offer an India pale lager. Bahr likes to dry hop his brews and then recirculate the mash as part of the process.

The brewery is new, and it looks new. New owners took a forty-year-old building and renovated it in beautiful fashion without skimping on authenticity. The former dark interior was brightened with skylights and large windows, a series of them overlooking the brewing process.

Bahr works with the chef to create dishes that highlight or utilize their beer. Patrons gather in the large beer hall at long tables to eat, drink, and listen to live music. There's a more private dining area, the King Gambrinus, on another side if that is more to your taste.

Up to 1,200 people can sit on the patio surrounded by fifteen acres of parkland and soccer fields.

BENJAMIN BEER COMPANY

507 Sixth St., Racine, WI 53403; (262) 583-2034; www.fit4denver.wixsite.com/benjaminbeer-launch

Founded: 2016 **Founder:** Jim Kennedy **Brewers:** Jim Kennedy and Matt Jung **Flagship beers:** Zombie Candy IPA, Belle City Blonde, Robust Porter, and American Pale Ale. **Seasonal beers:** Oktoberfest, Imperial Stout, Spring Nelson Sauvin IPA, and Summer Wheat. **Taproom hours:** Tues through Thurs, 4:30 to 9 p.m.; Fri, 4:30 to 11 p.m.; Sat, 11 a.m. to 11 p.m., and Sun, 11 a.m. to 9 p.m.

Technically, Jim Kennedy has done this before. The Benjamin Beer Company started brew life in Paddock Lake but moved to Racine almost exactly a year later.

They seem to be fitting in well across the street from the Indian Motor Co. motorcycle dealer. If neighbors take inspiration from what Kennedy has done, expect the stores on Sixth Street to brighten up. He's kept the vintage look of the building but brightened it with neutral color, contemporary barn doors, and a space to play board games near the brewhouse.

But you care about the beer, right? The **Zombie Candy IPA** is a delicious choice for hop heads. On a chilly afternoon, the **Robust Porter** warms from the inside.

They don't serve food here, but they do offer a Saturday music series with live performances.

BIG HEAD BREWING

6204 W. State St., Wauwatosa, WI 53213; (414) 257-9782; bigheadbrewingco.com

Founded: 2013 **Founder:** Patrick Fisher (Maria Kerrigan is a recent partner) **Brewer:** Rich Grose **Flagship beers:** Firefly IPA, SmASH ale, and Blonde **Tours:** By request **Taproom hours:** Wed through Fri, 4 to 10 p.m. and Sat, 1 to 11 p.m.

How convenient to have a cross-fit gym steps away from a brewery. More convenient is the luxury apartment complex across the street—actually three separate complexes. Or the location on a thoroughfare that gets jammed with quitting-time traffic, some of whom are employees who have just punched out from Miller Brewing, a little more than a mile east.

Thirst and convenience are reasons to stop here. My friend Mary enjoyed the **Sour Apple Grand Cru**. The apple is pronounced and she noted hints of apple pie spice. The only way to top that is with free games like pinball and table-top shuffleboard.

Founder Patrick Fisher calls it a "community center atmosphere." You are encouraged to bring your own food. Metcalfe's Market is conveniently located within walking distance. Pick up something from the deli. Know that once a week (or more) you'll find a party celebrating a birthday or other special occasion.

BILOBA BREWING

2970 N. Brookfield Rd., Brookfield, WI 53045; (262) 309-5820; bilobabrewing.com

Founded: 2014 **Founders:** Jean Lane and Gordon Lane **Brewers:** Kristen Giljohann and Gordon Lane **Taproom hours:** Thurs, 5:30 to 9:30 p.m.; Fri, 5 to 10:30 p.m.; and Sat 1 to 6 p.m.

The Lane family can blame themselves for Biloba's move. The fans demanded it. Biloba quickly outgrew the 500-square-foot taproom and 1 1/2-barrel system its first year in business, but stayed in its cozy spot for the sake of the regulars. Then, a vacancy showed up across the street and no one could argue when, in October of 2016, Biloba moved lock, stock, and barrel-aged brews to a new facility with its 1,500-square-foot taproom and a 10-barrel brewing system.

While the first Biloba site was deceiving (it resembled a dentist office from the outside more than a cozy brewery taproom), patrons can clearly find the new fieldstone brewery with its distinctive silo. The 1946 building, which was originally office space for the village of Brookfield, has three fireplaces inside. There may or may not be a television hidden behind sliding

NIGHT OUT STOUT

Style: Russian Imperial Stout

ABV: 13 percent

Availability: Limited on tap and in bottles

I still have a bottle of Biloba Brewing's **Night Out Stout**, a Russian Imperial breakfast stout aged in bourbon barrels, in my basement. It's from 2015 when they first introduced the brew. I take it out to look at it, then I put it back. There will be an occasion, a lottery ticket with half a chance, a snow storm where I could sip it with fresh oatmeal cookies, a spectacular day at work where I feel like I've earned time with this boozy beer mellowed with time but still packing a powerful punch. And then I will drink it and be sorry it's gone.

doors. The folks at Biloba prefer that you talk to each other, but this is Wisconsin and home of the Packers. Churches have been known to change their worship schedule during playoff seasons.

Biloba is a family operation. You'll often find Jean Lane behind the bar, daughter Kristen Griljohann brews, and daughter Kathryn Glomski is in charge of marketing. Gordon Lane is president and chief operating officer of Briess Malt & Ingredients Co. in Chilton, so he has more than a passing knowledge of brewing.

Gordon and Jean modeled Biloba after breweries in Portland. They wanted a place that was more like a coffee house or gathering place than a bar. In fact, Biloba draws families who play games, order pizza from a nearby restaurant, or just hang out. Others come for bottle releases like the **Night Out** barrel-aged stout or, as they did last year, to see how hops change the taste of a beer. The "hoptomist" series let beer lovers try the same style beer with different hops. They don't designate any of their beers as "flagship," but you'll usually find their **Section 25**, **Rye of the Wort**, **Smokin' Gramma**, **Golden Ale**, and **Saison on Oak** on tap.

Gordon Lane says the brewery has "a really good group of customers." You can be one.

BLACK HUSKY BREWING

909 E. Locust St., Milwaukee, WI 53212; (414) 509-8855; blackhuskybrewing.com

Founded: 2006 **Founders:** Toni Eichinger and Tim Eichinger **Brewer:** Tim Eichinger **Flagship beers:** Pale Ale and Sproose Joose IPA made with spruce tips **Seasonal beers:** Big Buck Brown, Deck Dog Honey Wheat, Jodlerkonig Oktoberfest, Milk Stout, and a Beware of the Dog series. **Tours:** Technical tours on Sun mornings **Taproom hours:** Sun, noon to 4 p.m.; Tues through Thurs, 3 to 9 p.m.; Fri, 3 to 10 p.m.; and Sat, 11 a.m. to 10 p.m.

It begins with the true, and often repeated, story of going out to the woods of Pembine, Wisconsin to get the tips off spruce trees for the flagship Sproose.

Toni and Tim started their brewery in a log cabin in front of their Northwoods home. It was quiet and private, but Tim would spend two days a week driving 200 miles one way to Milwaukee then Madison to deliver beer.

In 2016, the couple opened a brewery in Milwaukee, their former hometown. They landed on a former automotive store in the city's tight-knit and diverse Riverwest neighborhood. That's the key word to Black Husky—neighborhood. When someone defaced the sign out front, a neighbor offered to clean it off. Patrons sit out front in all weather, warmed by a bonfire when the weather chills.

Inside Black Husky, the Northwoods the Eichingers left behind are represented in the bar and a larger-than-life statue of their beloved husky, Howler, that an artist carved with a chainsaw.

Like Howler, Black Husky beers loom big, full of flavor and typically an ABV above 7 percent. There is usually a story about each beer.

Admire the 10-barrel brewhouse through the wall of windows to the east. Another window leads to the office where Smokey, the husky, waits patiently for her turn on the patio. Grab a seat in a club chair, admire the baby grand piano, or join the impromptu party. When Tim and Toni released Imperial **IPA Sparkly Eyes** as part of their Beware of the Dog series, a

SPROOSE II IPA

Style: American Double IPA

ABV: 8.6 percent

Availability: Year-round in bottles and on tap

Tim Eichinger throws real spruce tips into his Black Husky Sproose. He's known for bold beers and his **Sproose II IPA** tops the category for bold, especially for a beer that isn't barrel aged. Smell the spruce. Taste the juniper. The taste is reinforced with a malty backbone. Oh yeah, you'll want another.

cowbell party broke out. The label on the bottle depicts Lothar, one of the huskies the Eichingers cared for, and a note that it features more cowbell. Now that guy dancing like Will Ferrell makes sense.

Order a beer for yourself and a bowl of water for your pooch. Dogs are welcome here.

BRENNER BREWING CO.

706 S. 5th St., Milwaukee, WI 53204; (414) 465-8469; brennerbrewing.com

Founded: 2014 **Founder:** Mike Brenner **Brewer:** Mike Brenner **Flagship beers:** City Fox Pale Ale and Butterfly Farts Citrus Ale **Tours:** Thurs, 6 p.m.; Fri, 2, 4, 6, and 8 p.m.; Sat, noon, 2, 4, 6, and 8 p.m.; Sun, noon and 2 p.m. **Taproom hours:** Thurs, 4 to 10 p.m.; Fri, noon to 11 p.m.; Sat, 11 a.m. to 11 p.m.; and Sun, 11 a.m. to 8 p.m.

Mike Brenner owned an art gallery in Milwaukee, but found that people seemed more interested in the free beer he served during gallery openings than in the art he exhibited. It wasn't quite that simple, but Brenner went back to school, which took him to Germany, where he learned even more about brewing.

When he opened his brewery on 5th Street in the Walker's Point neighborhood, he was the only brewery in sight. Today, two others flank him on either end of the street. But Brenner is the only one connected to artists' studios. That part Brenner never gave up. Beer labels are designed by artists who are credited for their work.

For Brenner, beer is about community spirit and the accessibility of art and beer. Each can be challenging. Brenner wants to bridge that. He's always switching up beers, but the style most associated with the brewery is the **Bacon Bomb Rauchbier**, which tastes smoky like bacon. And **Butterfly Farts** because the beer has all the elements or a wheat brew, but possesses a sweet aftertaste that feels like summer. And then there's the name. Go ahead, order it without giggling.

The taproom hosts potluck parties for Packer games. Stick around until closing and there's a chance you'll see the brewer sing. It's happened before.

BROKEN BAT BREWING COMPANY

231 E. Buffalo St., Milwaukee, WI 53202; (414) 640-2269; facebook.com/BrokenBatBrewingCompany
Hours: Thurs, noon to 8 p.m.; Fri and Sat, noon to midnight; Sun, 11 a.m. to 7 p.m.

When you're obsessed with beer and baseball, you open a brewery with a baseball theme. That was the story for the owners of Broken Bat Brewing. Tim Pauly works for a baseball apparel company, Dan McElwee works for Carharrt. They turned that interest into a brewery in Milwaukee's Historic Third Ward. The district is stuffed with boutiques and restaurants, but Broken Bat is the first brewery there. Pauly and McElwee specialize in West Coast IPAs.

CITY LIGHTS

2210 W. Mount Vernon Ave., Milwaukee, WI 53233; (414) 436-1011; citylightsbrewing.com

Robin Gohsman and his son Jimmy Gohsman turned big plans into reality. City Lights is set in the former Milwaukee Gaslight building, designed by noted architect Alexander Eschweiler in the beginning of the twentieth century. It is one of two breweries in Milwaukee's Menomonee Valley, once the home of the city's stockyards, rendering plants, and other heavy industry. The area's renewal includes the high-rise Potawatomi Casino and Hotel, headquarters for Rishi Tea, and an Urban Ecology Center.

Patrons are able to view brewery production from the tasting room at the bottom of the stairs that lead to the formidable tower overhead (currently vacant). The Gohsmans can beer and fill kegs in the production area next door. They bring beer experience to the table, as in the Goshman brothers who once made and bottled blended beers.

COMPANY BREWING

735 E. Center St., Milwaukee, WI 53212; (414) 930-0909; companybrewing.com
Founded: 2015 **Founder:** George Bregar **Brewer:** George Bregar **Flagship beer:** Oaky Doke Red Ale **Seasonal beer:** Riverwest Backyard Hops **Taproom hours:** Tues through Sat, 4 p.m. to close; Sun, 10 a.m. for brunch to 2 p.m.

George Bregar, former coffee director for Milwaukee's Colectivo Coffee Roasters, made everyone forget the two brewpubs that lived in Company Brewing's spot before it. Hard to do in a neighborhood as tight as Riverwest, where Company Brewing resides. Bregar did it with great beer and delicious food. And music. Let's not forget the live music shows.

The décor is sparse but smart. Sit in the window to watch street life go by, or at the bar to watch the kitchen work sending out pub food that raises the bar on all other pub food.

Bregar consistently pumps out tasty beers such as the **HighLo Pale Ale** or the **Bounce House Wheat.** A personal favorite was the **Pomp and Pamplemousse,** a grapefruit IPA I still crave.

Company Brewing was first to host Milwaukee's Barley to Barrel incubator program, helping wannabe brewers get from concept to a concrete building.

It also hosts an annual neighborhood hops harvest. Everyone brings in his backyard hops and Bregar creates Riverwest Backyard Hops at the end of each summer using a wide variety of hops, some identifiable and some whose origin is unclear. There's a lot going on in that one beer. He makes it work.

DELAFIELD BREWHAUS

3832 Hillside Dr., Delafield, WI 53018; (262) 646-7821; delafield-brewhaus.com

Founded: 1999 **Founders:** Local investor group **Brewer:** John Harrison **Flagship beers:** Delafield Amber, Dockside Ale, Sommerzeit Hefeweizen, Pewaukee Porter, and Naga-Wicked Pale Ale. **Seasonal beers:** Mango Sunset Lager, Golden Promise British Ale, Bengal Bay Citra IPA, Millennium Tripel, Okterberfest, Forgotten Fermenter Imperial IPA, and Saphi Pilsner. **Taproom/restaurant hours:** Mon through Sat, 11 a.m. to 10 p.m.; Sun, 9 a.m. to 9 p.m.

"When we first opened, I couldn't serve a pale ale to save my life," brewer John Harrison said. Customers clamored for ambers. Amber remains popular, but the beer drinkers have expanded their palates. In return, Harrison has offered more styles and is perfecting those already on the roster. Now, his pale ale might have German malts or hard-to-find hops.

His fruit beers, such as his **Mango Sunset Lager,** are blended with real fruit juice because if you're going to offer a fruit beer, it should be natural. But he won't offer a sour. Brewing sour would be dangerous in the small but efficient brewhouse that Harrison designed in three floors. The odds of infection are more than Harrison wants to gamble with.

The bottom floor is for grains, milling, the boiler, and barrel-aging. The main floor, which customers see, is the brewing level. Lift your head to see the serving tanks, intentionally put up high so gravity does the work of dispensing the beer.

Foods in the expansive Delafield Brewhaus are paired with and made with beers. The brisket is infused with the **8-Ball Stout.**

Harrison was among the first in the Midwest to barrel-age beers. Two decades later, he's still putting beer in whiskey barrels. The week of Thanksgiving, regulars expect **Czar's Choice Russian Imperial Stout, Old No. 27 Barleywine,** and the **Wee Heavy Okauchee Scotchie.** Most of these have been swimming in whiskey barrels for at least a year.

Each autumn Delafield Brewhaus hosts the Schnapps Hans Cup (schnapphanscup.com), a home brew competition that draws contestants from across the country.

DISTRICT 14 BREWERY AND PUB

2273 S. Howell Ave., Milwaukee, WI 53207; (414) 744-0399; d14beer.com

Founded: 2014 **Founder:** Matt McCulloch **Brewer:** Matt McCulloch

Flagship beers: Always trying new small-batch creative craft brews

Taproom hours: Tues through Thurs, 3 p.m. to midnight; Fri, 3 p.m. to 2 a.m.; Sat noon to 2 a.m.; Sun, noon to midnight.

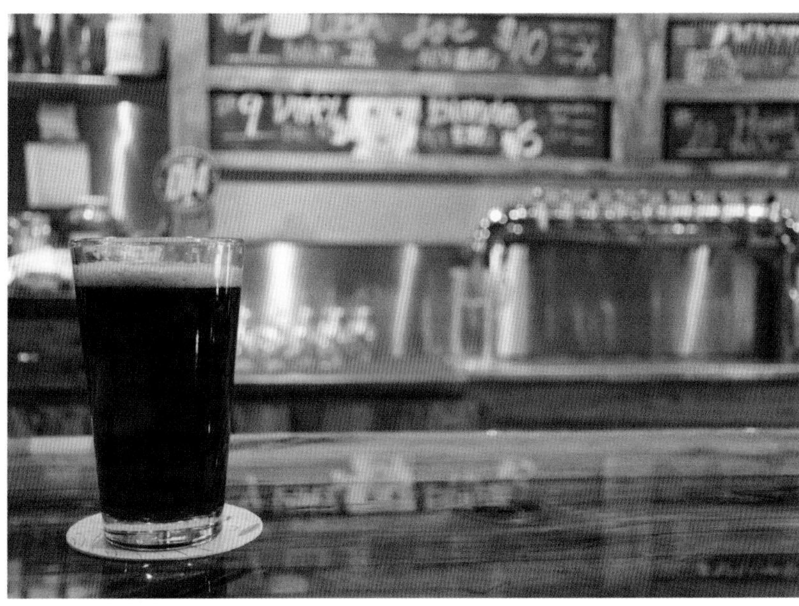

From the beginning, Matt McCulloch warned that he rarely makes the same beer twice. A bar full of beer drinkers seem better than okay with that.

It's easy to watch McCulloch at work. The brewhouse has a window for watching, but the door is also open. A pint of the **Miss Cleo ESB** goes down well with the fresh popcorn in a basket on the bar. The same could be said for the **Baggywrinkle Pale Ale** and the **Super Awesome Nameless Brown.**

D14, as people call it, is anchored in a busy stretch of Milwaukee's Bay View neighborhood. It's become the place to stop for a beer before heading out to eat, just as McCulloch intended. It's also the place to stop for a pizza (he serves them) or a drink after a meal. Cafe Lulu right next door is excellent.

ENLIGHTENED BREWING COMPANY

2918 S. 1st St., Milwaukee, WI 53207; enlightenedbeer@gmail.com; enlightenedbeer.com

Founded: 2014 **Founder:** Tommy Vandervort **Brewer and director of operations:** James Larson **Flagship beers:** A Priori pale ale and The Human Condition farmhouse ale. **Seasonal beers:** Daily Stipend pale wheat, Sustained Thought coffee stout. **Taproom hours:** Fri and Sat, 3 p.m. to midnight (subject to change with the season).

There's no need for a tour of the brewery. Patrons at the bar face it like it's on stage. In 2016, Tommy Vandervort and James Larson enlarged a tiny brewery, moving it down a flight from the second floor. Enlightened went from a 1/2-barrel operation in a 500-square-foot area to a 3 1/2-barrel system with space for a taproom.

There are more beers and, lucky you, they're all good. Oh, the thoughts you'll have with the rich **Sustained Thought** milk stout. Actually, you'll just be thinking about possibly ordering another.

Larson calls the complex around Enlightened a "little bee hive." Neighbors include the Dock 18 Cocktail Lab. The fancy name refers to the guys who started the handcrafted bitters company, Bittercube Bitters, that changed the way the Midwest looks at craft cocktails from Minneapolis to Milwaukee. Another is Top Note Tonic. The bottom line is, you'll never go thirsty here.

The taproom's design was constructed so "everything is visible without a barrier," Vandervort said. They wanted customers to enjoy the sights and smells of a brewery. If the garage doors are open, then they are, too.

"One or two of the flagship beers will always be on tap," Larson said. But they'll try other things as well.

Vandervort and Larson started small and sent their beers out to a handful of Milwaukee bars before beginning the expansion. The idea was to grow organically even if that meant digging the brewery's trench themselves.

Visit expecting to chat about beer. but don't go thinking the game is on. There is no plan to add a television. Vandervort and Larson want customers to talk to each other, solve the world's problems, or enjoy a game of cribbage.

The patio is open when the weather obliges. Enlightened is dog-friendly. Well, dog-friendly to dogs who are human-friendly, Larson quips.

EXPLORIUM BREWPUB

5300 S. 76th St., Suite 1450A, Greendale, WI 53129; (813) 240-9455; exploriumbrew.com

There was always something missing at Southridge Mall in the historic Village of Greendale. It begged for a place to get a fresh-brewed beer and a bite to eat. Not anymore. Owner Mike Doble, an engineering consultant and building designer, fixed that problem by opening Explorium Brewpub with twenty-four house taps made onsite.

Doble has beer in his genetics. Doble's family runs Tampa Bay Brewing Company in Florida. His brother Mark owns Aviator Brewing in Raleigh, North Carolina, and a cousin owns Outer Banks Brewing Station, a brewpub in Kill Devil Hills, North Carolina. We can't wait to see what Doble does.

THE FERMENTORIUM

7481 Hwy. 60, Cedarburg, WI 53012; (262) 421-8593; thefermentorium.com
Founded: 2016 **Founders:** Kris Volkmann **Brewer:** David Kelley
Flagship beer: Covered Bridge Golden Ale and Safe Passage Porter
Taproom hours: Wed and Thurs, 4 to 10 p.m.; Fri. and Sat, noon to 10 p.m.; Sun, noon to 6 p.m.

Covered Bridge Golden Ale is The Fermentorium's homage to the last covered bridge in Wisconsin, located right down the road from the brewery. The beers here are divided into series, and Covered Bridge is part of the traditional series. The Hop Wheel series is for the hop-forward beer drinkers and includes brews such as a Manoomin, a summer English Double IPA with English Bramling Cross hops. Brewer's Reserve is for the

more adventurous beer styles and includes brew such as the **Fou D'Amour,** a spiced Belgian blonde and malty **Whispering Scythe.** A farm-to-glass series and a barrel-aged series are also on tap.

Plop down on a leather sofa or play free table-top Atari, this brewery is a something-for-everyone kind of place. The bar is made of reclaimed wood that gives the store-like setting (this used to be a pet store) an industrial chic look. That doesn't explain the Scourge of Carpathia guarding the restrooms, however.

Long public tables are meant for sharing a pint and a conversation. It's the same at the bar where the bartender dispenses peanuts or a spicy snack mix for $1. You'll need a sip of the double IPA after that. They don't serve food in the tasting room but you can bring your own or order from the drive-in down the road.

GATHERING PLACE BREWING COMPANY

811 E. Vienna Ave., Milwaukee, WI 53212; gatheringplacebrewing.com

After winning several awards for his home brews, Joe Yeado, a senior researcher at the Public Policy Forum, brought his beer to the public with Gathering Place and opened the third spot for beer in Milwaukee's Riverwest neighborhood. His tap list includes dubbles, milk stouts, pale ales, and German hefeweizens along with seasonal brews and one-off beers available only in the taproom. He chose the name Gathering Place to reflect the community involvement he hopes for breweries. The taproom will be open to the public beginning in late June 2017.

GOOD CITY BREWING

2108 N. Farwell Ave., Milwaukee, WI 53202; (414) 539-4343; goodcitybrewing.com

Founded: 2016 **Founders:** Andy Jones, David Dupee, and Dan Katt **Brewer:** Andy Jones **Flagship beers:** Motto Mosaic Pale Ale, Good City Pils, Risk IPA, and Reward Double IPA **Seasonal beers:** Density Imperial Stout **Taproom hours:** Tues and Wed, 4 p.m. to midnight; Thurs through Sat, 11:30 a.m. to midnight; Sun, 11:30 a.m. to 10 p.m.

Beer or food, that's the question. The answer is both.

Beer might be the star of the show here. It's in the name. But the food is its match, from the Vegetable Laska to the curry fries.

REWARD

Style: Imperial IPA

ABV: 8.5 percent

Availability: Year-round and by crowler

Risk is Good City Brewing's traditional IPA. **Reward** is its bigger, bolder brother that is the reward to the end of a work day. It's filled with Eureka, Citra, and Amarillo hops, which create a pineapple character backed with a chorus of floral, lemon-citrus hop flavor. It goes deliciously with the curry fries. Sit by the fire. Sip. enjoy.

The founders wanted to put down roots as a neighborhood brewery. They transformed a former bike shop on a busy urban street into a beer oasis. In the summer, patrons can sit by windows that open to the world or choose a people-watching seat on the sidewalk. When temperatures drop, as they always do in Milwaukee, patrons warm themselves near the gas fireplace in the taproom. I recommend a **Density Imperial Stout** for just such an occasion. Its warm, roasty, almost burnt, coffee taste can take the chill off.

The brewery is visible from nearly every seat in the house and along the way to the restrooms. Lucky are those who can watch Andy Jones fill a cask with the likes of their **Dapper British Session Ale.**

Those who sit at the counter can watch the magic of the crowler machine as it sends out beer to go.

And when you're done, you can walk off any calories with a trip to the Oriental Theater, a 1927 movie palace decorated in East Indian style and artifacts. The Oriental still uses a Kimball theater pipe organ tucked under the stage.

HOPS & LEISURE

1225 Robruck Dr., Oconomowoc, WI 53066; (262) 567-8536; hopsandleisure.com

Founded: 2015 **Founders:** Al Leofilos **Brewer:** John Harrison at Delafield Brewhaus **Flagship beers:** Dr. Leisure Pale Ale, Leisureologist Dark Ale Porter, Leisure Kolsch, and Leisure Amber **Taproom hours:** Mon through Sat, 11 a.m. to 11 p.m.; Sun, 11 a.m. to 10 p.m.

It's a wonder someone didn't think of this brewpub name before. It explains perfectly how beer appreciation is both mouth-watering and relaxing. The beers here are solid and the food is good. Try the fish tacos, you'll swear you are in California. At least until you reach the outdoors.

Hops & Leisure has a large patio on the side of the building, which defies its paved-over-shopping-mall location and is the perfect place to enjoy their **Dr. Leisure Pale Ale** and **Leisure Amber,** which is brewed at Delafield Brewhaus.

LAKEFRONT BREWING

1872 N. Commerce St., Milwaukee, WI 53212; (414) 372-8800; lakefrontbrewery.com

Founded: 1987 **Founders:** Russ Klisch, Jim Klisch, and Carson Praefke **Brewer:** Marc Luther Paul **Flagship beers:** Riverwest Stein, New Grist (gluten free) and Eye PA, IPA **Tours:** Mon, noon to 4 p.m.; Tues through Thurs, noon to 7 p.m.; Fri, noon to 8 p.m.; Sat, 11 a.m. to 8 p.m.; Sun, noon to 2 p.m. Check the website for mini-tour times. Technical tours are offered on Sun. **Taproom hours:** Mon through Thurs, 11 a.m. to 8 p.m.; Fri, 11 a.m. to 9 p.m.; Sat, 9 a.m. to 9 p.m., Sun, 10 a.m. to 5 p.m.

Everything here is Milwaukee. It's true. Jim and Russ Klisch are Milwaukee-born. Sibling rivalry over who could make the best home brew is the brewery's foundation.

The building is the former Milwaukee Electric Railway and Light Company's coal-fired power plant. The Arts and Crafts lights hanging from the tall ceiling are museum pieces, really. Lakefront acquired these lights, salvaged from the long-gone Plankinton Hotel, in an online auction with a $5,013 bid for all twelve lights. Even though the brothers were outbid by a guy from Chicago who offered $10,000, the city wanted the lights to stay home and honored Lakefront's lower bid.

The lights aren't the only pieces of history here, though. The oversized beer mug where tours begin is from the old County Stadium ballpark where the Major League Milwaukee Brewers played before moving to Miller Park. Balloons would be released from the mug for every home run. The food booth on the patio along the Milwaukee River spent an earlier life as a chalet for the team's mascot at County Stadium.

Even the tours are Milwaukee. Where else would groups be forced to sing the theme song to *Laverne & Shirley,* a sitcom set at a fictional brewery in Milwaukee. Pints flow. Guides make jokes about the brewing process, and everyone yells the word "bung hole" at least once during the

RIVERWEST STEIN

ABV: 5.6 percent

Availability: Year-round

Named for the Milwaukee neighborhood where it was founded, **Riverwest Stein** is the classic Lakefront go-to brew and, when it doubt about what to order, I order this. It pours a deep amber color. American hops give it bitterness but the German lager yeast makes it a great companion for schnitzel.

forty-five-minute tour. Lakefront's tours have been ranked among the best in the country, as much for the fun as the amount of beer offered on the tour.

The brewery was designed much like a German beer hall. On Friday nights, the long tables are shared by diners getting a fish fry (they also serve pretzels and fried cheese curds, so Milwaukee).

Lakefront was among the first craft breweries in Milwaukee and is credited as the second brewery in the country to produce pumpkin beer and one of the first to offer a gluten-free brew with its **New Grist.**

Lakefront also collaborated with a Milwaukee-based non-profit that provides sustainable vegetables and protein for inner city residents to create **Growing Power Farmhouse Pale Ale,** a Belgian-style beer made with organic barley and organic hops.

There's more. Lakefront was the first brewery in the state to be certified travel green by Travel Green Wisconsin.

But it's the beer that is the biggest draw. Each Friday after Thanksgiving people stand in long lines, often in sub-zero temperatures, to get a bottle or two of the brewery's **Black Friday** beer, typically a barrel-aged stout. This Black Friday event has become a post-Thanksgiving tradition.

LIKE MINDS BREWING

823 E. Hamilton Ave., Milwaukee, WI 53202; (414) 239-8587; likemindsbrewing.com

Founded: 2016 **Founders:** Justin Aprahamian and John Lavelle **Brewer:** John Lavelle **Flagship beers:** Sour Rhubarb Saison, Flora Sour Brown, Exiled Wheat Saison, Horehound Double IPA, Nighthawks Oatmeal Stout, and Archimedes Brett IPA **Taproom hours:** Tues through Sat, 4 to 10 p.m. for food, midnight for beer.

It was a twisty road for Like Minds opening in Milwaukee. The highlights: Wisconsin suggests the brewery go to Illinois. Like Minds sets up in Chicago. Wisconsin decides, well, maybe they should be in the state. Like Minds opens a second brewery in Milwaukee.

It's a more complicated story than that, but the ending is still happy. After many nights of brewing beer together, Justin Aprahamian, a James Beard award–winning chef and owner of the highly regarded Sanford restaurant, and John Lavelle, who created the Beer Fridge app, combined forces to create beer recipes.

Like Minds brewed at Hinterland Brewing in Green Bay for a while but decided to start a brewery at home in Milwaukee in 2015. However, state law forbids anyone who owns a tavern or restaurant, as Aprahamian does, or retail liquor store from obtaining a permit for a brewery.

Like Minds found a location in Chicago near the United Center and blocks from Goose Island and opened their brewery. Lavelle would make the drive, his car loaded with charred fruit for the brewery's sours. Then the Wisconsin Department of Revenue had a change of heart and Like Minds opened a brewery and restaurant in walking distance of Sanford in October 2015, though they still brew in Chicago.

You don't need to know all this to visit Like Minds, but it helps to understand. If they put this much effort into getting a brewery, imagine how the beer tastes.

The Milwaukee location is a light-filled space thanks in part to a skylight in the center of the dining room. Tables are long and simple but sophisticated. The brewery is visible through a large glass window at the end of the hallway where the restrooms are located. The food menu is elegant bar food, such as corn dogs with barley malt ketchup and mustard.

Take a seat at the bar. Order an **Archimedes** to appreciate what Brettanomyces can add to an IPA.

ARCHIMEDES BRETT IPA

Style: India Pale Ale

ABV: 6.5 percent

Availability: Year-round

The newish Like Minds Brewery takes IPA one step farther by adding Brettanomyces yeast to an already perfect IPA. You'll taste grapefruit and other citrus notes inside but the finish is all IPA.

MILLERCOORS BREWING

4251 W. State St., Milwaukee, WI 53208; (414) 931-2337; millercoors.com/breweries/miller-brewing-company/tours/tour-information

Founded: 1855 **Founder:** Frederick J. Miller **Flagship beers:** Miller Genuine Draft, Miller High Life, Miller Lite **Tours:** Mon through Sat, every 30 minutes, 10:30 a.m. to 3:30 p.m.; Sun, 10:30 a.m. to 2 p.m. Seasonal hours apply. See the website.

Much of the story of Milwaukee is in the MillerCoors tour. The tour begins with the Girl in the Moon story and ends with free samples in the Miller Inn.

I drive through the Miller Valley and through the MillerCoors campus each day on the way to and from work. It's a cruise through history past what used to be the Gettleman Brewery (now the Miller gym), past the former horse stables and the Miller Caves. Cases of beer seem to defy gravity as they cross the street on a skywalk conveyor that connects one side of campus to the other.

Oh, those Miller Caves. Chilled with lake ice, the caves are where Frederick J. Miller lagered his beers. They were closed in 1906 but opened again in 1953 by Frederick C. Miller, grandson to the founder. Liberace was there for the ribbon cutting. A hologram of Frederick J. Miller, the founder, welcomes you to the caves. It's both freaky and a feat of technology.

Even if you think you know everything there is to know about beer, take the tour. The view of a macro-brewery at work offers perspective for craft brewery tours. The fact that hundreds of people make the same beer and make it taste consistently the same every single time is a study in production. You'll go up steps and down steps, so be prepared.

Also be prepared to marvel at the size of the brew kettles. They are large enough to fill a stadium.

There are plenty of samples to taste at the end of the tour in the Miller Inn or on the patio across the street when the weather allows. Miller used to give its guests post cards to fill out and send out like proper tourists. I wish they still did that.

MillerCoors sometimes hosts Brewers Unleashed at the brewery in which brewers from other MillerCoors locations are introduced to Milwaukee audiences. That sometimes includes brewers from the Tenth Street Brewery across town. Food is included and the events are free.

More recently, the pilot brewery and Chicago's Off Color brewing collaborated on a beer for Off Color. It was a first, perhaps, but likely not a last.

The Miller Caves recently opened for invitation-only dinners. It's an old tradition started by Frederick C. Miller. A different restaurant chef prepares appetizers paired to beers in the MillerCoors portfolio, including some that aren't sold publicly. MillerCoors also offers a musical light show beginning at the Plank Road Brewery and stopping at the MillerCoors guest center during the holidays. Sign up to walk the tour or enjoy it from the warmth of a vehicle.

MILWAUKEE BREWING COMPANY

1131 N. 8th St., Milwaukee, WI and 613 S. 2nd St., Milwaukee, WI 53204; mkebrewing.com

Founded: 1997 **Founders:** Jim McCabe and Mike Brieser **Brewer:** Robert Morton **Flagship beers:** Louie's Demise Alt Amber, Sheepshead Stout, Hop Happy IPA, Booyah Apricot Saison, and Outboard Cream Ale **Seasonal beer:** Sasquash **Tours:** Fri, between 4 and 6:30 p.m. on the half hour; Sat, between 1 and 4 p.m. on the half hour. Open house tours are Sat at 5 p.m. They last two hours and cost more. Sunday tours are given at 2, 3, and 4 p.m. June through September. **Taproom hours:** Open daily at 11 a.m.

The information is complicated—for now. Pay attention. Milwaukee Brewing Co., is in the process of moving to the former Pabst Brewing distribution center, one of the last buildings to be redeveloped on the campus. Pabst closed in 1996.

Visitors to the renovated 50,000-square-foot location can expect a taproom, restaurant, gift shop, and "a rooftop experience," as owner Jim

McCabe calls it, from a rooftop bar that will overlook the city's skyline. Later in 2017, production will be moved to the new location.

Then, in 2018, the Pabst location will find itself at the edge of the Milwaukee Bucks' new arena and proposed entertainment center. Yup, Milwaukee Brewing for the win.

McCabe said they will keep the 613 S. 2nd St., location and continue tours there until production is moved. Once production moves to the former Pabst campus, the 2nd Street brewery will become a pilot brewery and a center for the brewery's award-winning, barrel-aged beer program and expanding sour beer production.

There's so much expansion it would be easy to overlook the beer. Don't do that. Brewer Robert Morton studied at the Culinary Institute of America, and it shows. **Hop Happy,** an IPA, includes oats in the mash. **Gin Barrel Aged O-Gii** is an Imperial Wit infused with organic green tea and ginger then aged in Rehorst Reserve gin barrel from Milwaukee-based Great Lakes Distillery. It won gold in the specialty/experimental category at the 2015 Festival of Barrel Aged Beers in Chicago. The seasonal **Sasquash** is an autumn beer made with 400 pounds of pumpkin and 300 pounds of sweet potato.

Another item to not overlook is the Milwaukee Ale House, the birthplace of the brand where beer is still made on a small scale. The Ale House serves as a tasting room for the 2nd Street location. The two-story complex has a restaurant and a selection of Milwaukee Brewing beers from which to choose. If the weather allows, sit on the deck, which has a river view and docks for thirsty boaters. The Midwinter Brewfest, a beer festival for charity, is held at the Ale House each February.

MOBCRAFT BEER

505 S. 5th St., Milwaukee, WI; (414) 488-2019; mobcraftbeer.com

Founded: 2012 **Founders:** Henry Schwartz, Giotto Troia, and Andrew Gierczak **Brewer:** Andrew Gierczak **Flagship beers:** Night and Day Vanilla Black Ale, Hop Gose the Grapefruit Wheat, and Bat Sh!t Crazy Coffee beer **Tours:** Sat and Sun, check website for times **Taproom hours:** Mon through Thurs, 3 to 10 p.m.; Fri, 3 p.m. to midnight; Sat, noon to midnight; and Sun, noon to 10 p.m.

You might recall MobCraft from such television shows as *Shark Tank.* Henry Schwartz presented the MobCraft model in spring 2016. Mark Cuban didn't go for their idea, but that hasn't slowed the MobCraft train at all.

MobCraft is crowd-sourced. Anyone of legal age can submit a recipe to be brewed. It can be as simple as "I want a beer that tastes like . . . " Or it can be a full recipe. Fans cast their votes on the beer to be brewed by placing a pre-order on it.

A trio of college friends started MobCraft in 2012. For a time they brewed beer at the House of Brews in Madison before finding a permanent location in Milwaukee.

Kudos to whomever thought to barrel age a dark sour and then add black cherries, blackberries, and apricots—all the food groups to create the delicious **Black Tart Outlaw.**

The taproom is a former motor repair shop that, in certain light, resembles artist Edward Hopper's *Nighthawks.* The bar is long and ends just as the windows to the brewery begin. Vintage furniture beckons. So does an outdoor patio set on the super-sized sidewalk.

Millennials own the place but other age groups hang out there. It's close enough to the Harley-Davidson Museum to be considered a biker hangout. It's also a watering hole for visitors to the Iron Horse Hotel, a renovated factory now serving as a hotel with fine dining, directly across the street.

MobCraft is one of three breweries on Milwaukee's 5th Street. There isn't an official walking tour of the three—MobCraft, Brenner Brewing, and Urban Harvest . . . yet.

PABST MILWAUKEE BREWERY

1037 W. Juneau Ave., Milwaukee, WI 53233
https://pabstmkebrewery.com/; Hours: Mon through Fri, open at 4 p.m.; Sat and Sun, open at 11 a.m.

When Pabst Brewery shut down twenty years ago, Milwaukee residents mourned. Frederick Pabst was a titan of the community who built a brewery campus on a hill looking east toward Lake Michigan. Eugene Kashper, chairman and chief executive officer of Pabst, renewed the brand on campus by opening an innovation brewery with restaurant and tasting room in a former church on the campus. His brewery pumps out Old Tankard (made for a while at Wisconsin Brewing in Verona), Kloster, and other pre-Prohibition recipes.

PUBLIC CRAFT BREWING CO.

716 58th St., Kenosha, WI 53140; (262) 652-2739; publiccraftbrewing.com
Founded: 2012 **Founder:** Matt Geary **Brewer:** Matt Geary **Flagship beer:** K-Town Brown **Taproom hours:** Tues through Fri, 3:30 to 9 p.m.; Sat, noon to 9 p.m.; Sun, noon to 6 p.m.

Beer is king but comfort isn't overlooked at Public Craft. A big comfortable chair is wedged next to a bookshelf for reading and sipping. Don't want to just sit? Fling metal discs across the shuffleboard, play foosball or a board game. Or, and this is key, use one of the several gel pens to create artwork on a Public Craft Brewing coaster, then record your mini-artwork on Instagram (it's encouraged!). While you're there, you might want to include a picture of the **Bits and Pieces** pale ale, too. Your friends will appreciate the recommendation. Oh yeah, and they play vinyl here. Customers sometimes leave their albums behind so they can listen to them on a return visit.

View the brewing process on a walk to the restrooms, and say "Hi" when a brewer walks out of the cooler as you're reading the many stickers on the wall from other popular breweries. Yes, let's "Keep Wisconsin beer'd."

The **K-Town Brown** is the most famous of Public's brews, but try the **Bone Dry Irish Stout** on Nitro, malts make it roasty and nitrogen makes it smooth. Ireland smooth.

Public Craft also hosts an open mic night one Thursday each month. There's a lot going on here.

R'NOGGIN BREWERY

6521 120th Ave., Kenosha, WI 53142; (262) 960-1298; rnogginbrewing.com/rstory.html
Founded: 2016 **Founders:** Kevin Bridleman and Jeff Bridleman **Brewers:** Kevin Bridleman and Jeff Bridleman **Flagship beers:** Cream Ale, Pale Ale, Brown Ale, and IPA Batch 1 **Taproom hours:** Fri, 6 to 10 p.m.

Two brewers equal two meanings for the name R'Noggin. According to co-founder Jeff Bridleman, a "noggin" is a 4-ounce pour. However, he also adds, "Customers are welcome to try beers created by our noggin."

Cars headed to the Illinois border breeze by R'Noggin one way, and those headed deeper into Wisconsin swoosh by the other way on Interstate 94. Slow down or miss an opportunity.

Jeff Bridleman is an architect. He and Kevin, who works in human resources consulting, spent three years looking for the best spot for the brewery. They found an unused garage on seven acres between two popular taverns—Rivals and Uncle Mike's Highway Pub and just up the road from Uke's Harley-Davidson. After clearing the woods, paving a driveway, and designing a two-story taproom for R'Noggin, the brothers cooked up **Batch No. 1** on the brewery's 2 1/2-barrel system, which was almost as challenging as designing the logo for the beer—a skeleton wearing a top hat and bow tie with two playing cards—numbers 2 and 7. Kevin explains that they wanted a Mad Hatter theme that was edgy. So much for the skeleton. He had to be a gambler, because the brewery is a gamble. And the number 27 is a recurring number for the family and had to be part of the logo. They combined everything perfectly—on both the logo and the brewery. On the day I visited, a group of ten riders on Harleys rumbled up to the tasting room, proving that, yup, the brewery was in exactly the right spot.

RAISED GRAIN BREWING COMPANY

2244 W. Bluemound Rd., Waukesha, WI 53186; (262) 505-5942; raisedgrainbrewing.com
Founded: 2015 **Founders:** Nick Reistad, Kevin Brandenburg, Scott Kelley, and James Gosset **Brewers:** Scott Kelley and James Gosset.
Flagship beers: Hop Doctor IPA, Paradocs Red Imperial IPA, Kilted Kolsch, Ah Ha IPA, Birdseye Belgian Tripel, and Six Stone Scotch Ale
Seasonal beer: Santa's Sack Christmas Ale **Tours:** Sat, 2 and 3 p.m.
Taproom hours: Thurs, 4 to 8 p.m.; Wed and Thurs, 4 to 10 p.m.; Fri, 3 p.m. to midnight; Sat, noon to midnight; Sun, 11:30 a.m. to 6:30 p.m.

It took one beer to become a believer. The **Black Walnut Brazilian Coffee Stout** is one of Raised Grain's experimental beers. It was one in a flight of Raised Grain beers. I also fell in love with the **Paradocs Red Imperial IPA** and the **Birdseye Belgian Tripel.** The doctors make good beer.

PARADOCS

Style: Red Imperial IPA

ABV: 8.7 percent

Don't come to Raised Grain expecting a light beer. **Paradocs,** which won gold at the 2016 North American Beer Awards, is on middle ground. It's not the biggest beer in the lineup. There's a bright hop aroma but also notes of caramel. You won't notice the ABV as it goes down.

Scott Kelley and James Gosset are practicing physicians. Kelley specializes in dermatophathology and Gosset is a vascular surgeon. They were home brewers who became professionals on a 7-barrel system in a strip mall near a brewery supply store and across the street from Home Depot. It's where the brewery calls home. Inside is decorated in reclaimed wood—a nod to the name as well as a business close to Reistad's heart. The lumber comes from the storied A.J. Pietsch Co., a woodworking shop on display at the Milwaukee Public Museum. The founders explain they chose the name because "we're a little rough around the edges."

That's a humble brag. Their beer wins awards and high marks from customers, some who come on Saturdays for the brewhouse yoga. For those not so concerned with fitness, flights come with some amazing pretzel bits—they're buttery and crunchy. But if they're not enough, a rotating assortment of food trucks are scheduled for weekends and special occasions.

RIVERSIDE BREWERY AND RESTAURANT

255 S. Main St., West Bend, WI 53095; (262) 334-2739; riversidebreweryandrestaurant.com/brews.shtml

Founded: 2005 **Founders:** Wayne Kainz and Dana Kainz **Brewer:** Scott Bartell **Flagship beer:** Main Street Amber Ale **Taproom hours:** Kitchen is open Mon through Thurs, 11 a.m. to 9 p.m.; Fri and Sat, 11 a.m. to 10 p.m.; Sun, 10 a.m. to 8 p.m.

This place is huge, and it fills up quickly. If tables are full downstairs, you can grab a seat at the bar upstairs and wait. The eight taps in front of you can help pass the time. Or, if the weather allows, grab a spot on the patio. This is the west bend of the river, from which the city took its name.

Beer styles here change frequently. Look for the **Dizzy Blonde Weiss, The Broken Oak Dubel,** or **The Emperor's New Stout,** with its hints of coffee and hops finish.

West Bend has a sweet downtown, but don't miss the Wisconsin Museum of Art on your way in. The contemporary-looking museum features some of the state's art treasures.

RUSTIC ROAD BREWING

510 56th St., Kenosha, WI 53140; (262) 320-7623; rusticbrewing.com
Founded: 2012 **Founder:** Greg York **Brewer:** Tom Stole **Flagship beer:** Rustic Road Hail to the Ale Amber Ale **Taproom hours:** Wed and Thurs, 5 to 10 p.m.; Fri, 4 p.m. to 1 a.m.; Sat, noon to 1 a.m.; Sun, noon to 5 p.m.

Founder Greg York calls his brewery a nanobrewer with a pub. See for yourself. Beer is made in the front window, much as it has been since the brewery opened in 2012. The shotgun shape of the brewery means it's

sometimes a tight squeeze between the tables across from the bar and the bags of grain in the back of the pub, but that just gives it a homey feel. And, it's easy to forget that Kenosha is a beach town, the brewery is a slight squint from lakefront viewing. There's something cool about having a beer in a place where a brewer is likely to walk by with a sack of grain for, I don't know, the **Rustic Road 60 Shilling Scottish Ale** perhaps.

ST. FRANCIS BREWING CO.

3825 S. Kinnickinnic Ave., St. Francis, WI 53235; (414) 744-4448; stfrancisbrewery.com/Beer.php
Founded: 2009 **Founder:** Copul Enterprises **Brewer:** Scott Hettig **Flagship beers:** Greed Session IPA, Lust Weissbier, Wrath Amber Ale, Envy IPA, and Sloth Brown Ale **Seasonal beers:** Gluttony and Pride **Taproom hours:** Sun, 10 a.m. to 9 p.m.; Mon through Thurs, 11 a.m. to 10 p.m.; and Fri and Sat, 11 a.m. to 11 p.m.

This place bustles. The parking lot fills up on Friday night with locals who demand a fish fry. The menu goes around the world from ribs to chicken schnitzel to bangers and mash to fettuccini. Most entrees are designed to go with one of the seven deadly sins, er, beers on tap. Ask the server or pick your own combination. The caramel and chocolate malts of **Wrath Amber Ale** pair well with the ribs.

SILVER CREEK BREWERY

N57 W6172 Portland Rd., Cedarburg, WI 53012; (262) 375-4444; silvercreekbrewing.com
Founded: Opened 2002 **Founders:** Steven Venturing and Todd Schneeberger **Flagship beers:** Hefe-Weiss, Porter **Seasonal beers:** Imperial Mai-Bock, Oktoberfest, Vintage Ale **Taproom hours:** Tues through Fri, 3 p.m. to around midnight; Sat, noon to around 1 a.m.; Sun: noon to 8 p.m.

Wait, did you take a wrong turn into Connecticut? Cedarburg is the definition of quaint, and Silver Creek Brewery takes full advantage. Travel past the Cedar Creek Settlement, a former woolen mill turned into a warren of artist studios, antique shops, and restaurants. Continue past the pagoda-shaped building and immediately south of the feed store is the unassuming pathway to the brewery. Unassuming at first glance, only. Look right to see the waterfalls pouring into the creek and left to open the sturdy doors of the former grist mill turned brewery.

Snuggle inside where the brewhouse is on full display. Play cribbage and sip a Porter while winter howls outside. And when the weather allows, head out to the waterside patio. Tourists compare the taproom and its 40-inch thick walls to English pubs. Televisions tuned to Badgers and Packers games remind you it's Wisconsin.

There will likely be a party going on around you when you visit. Cedarburg hosts several seasonal festivals, including a wine and harvest fest, Oktoberfest (the brewery has a beer for that), a strawberry festival, and a winter festival. Each spring the community also celebrates with a beer festival. The calendar is listed at cedarburgfestival.org.

SPRECHER BREWING COMPANY

701 W. Glendale Ave., Glendale, WI 53209; (414) 964-2379; sprecherbrewery.com/index.php
Founded: 1985 **Founder:** Randal Sprecher **Brewmaster:** Craig Burge **Flagship beers:** Black Bavarian and Special Amber **Seasonal beers:** Oktoberfest, Winterbrew, Mai Bock, and Summer Pils **Tours:** Mon through Thurs, 4 p.m.; Fri, 3 and 4 p.m.; Sat, noon to 5:15 p.m.; Sun 11 a.m.- 5 p.m.; subject to change seasonally **Taproom hours:** Mon through Sat, 11 a.m. to 6 p.m.; Sun, 11 a.m. to 5 p.m.

Randy Sprecher started Milwaukee's craft beer movement. He left his job at Pabst Brewery and launched his own brewery where he emphasized European-style beers such as the Schwarzbier-style **Black Bavarian.** Milwaukee thanks him. Sprecher Brewing was actually Milwaukee's first craft brewery since Prohibition. Opened in 1985 in a three-story building at a different location, the brewery offered **Black Bavarian, Special Amber,** and **Milwaukee Pils.**

They continue the tradition now on Glendale Avenue, and everyone gets involved. Sprecher is a family business: Randy is the brewery's CEO; daughter Kecia is in charge of graphics and packaging; and Anne, Randy's wife of twelve years, heads up communications and social media.

Tours are popular, so it's wise to book in advance. The tours don't filter through the entire brewery but give you enough of a glimpse to get the feel for the quantity of beverages made here. Sprecher was among the first to introduce handcrafted sodas and debuted **Sprecher Root Beer** in 1989. More than half the brewery's sales come from root beer and soda.

BLACK BAVARIAN

Style: Schwarzbier

ABV: 5.8 percent

Availability: Year-round in bottles and on tap

Smell the black licorice. Taste the molasses. There's a roastiness, but not an overwhelming one in Sprecher's Black Bavarian. A highly-rated American Schwarzbier, Randal Sprecher calls it his favorite.

It was also among the first to brew hard root beer, a fermented malt beverage that turns the popular root beer into an adults-only beverage. Don't skip the beer, though. On my visit, Craig Burge was taste-testing a blueberry lambic straight from the tank, something he does with each beer. And he knows what is in each marked and unmarked tank. Try the **Magnum Pale Ale,** made with Magnum and Cascade hops from Wisconsin.

Adults can try one beer on the tour, while those younger than twenty-one can try a soda. The tour concludes at the tasting room—a paneled room covered by a huge white tent in Oktoberfest style. An oversized half barrel anchors one end of the room and picnic tables encourage visitors to chat with each other or maybe share a bag of Sprecher potato chips.

In summer, Sprecher brings out a fleet of emergency vehicles that have been reconfigured to serve beer. The fleet anchors the Milwaukee County Parks' Traveling Beer Garden. The vehicles visit county parks for two weeks at a time dispensing beer, soda, and snacks.

SWEET MULLETS BREWING COMPANY

N58 W39800 Industrial Rd., Suite D, Oconomowoc, WI 53066; (262) 456-2843; sweetmulletsbrewing.com

Founded: 2012 **Founder:** Chad Ostram bought the brewery and reopened it in 2016. **Brewer:** Chad Ostram **Flagship beer:** Jorge **Tours:** Every second and fourth Sat, 12:20 and 2 p.m. **Taproom:** Mon, Wed, and Thur, 4 to 10 p.m.; Sat, 12 to 8 p.m.; Sun, 11:30 a.m. to 9 p.m.

It's a rainy Saturday afternoon and Sweet Mullets is pouring a lot of beer. Boat culture is big in Oconomowoc. Boaters stop here to fill up before they hit the water and stop back in for dinner and a brew on the way home. Apparently they also stop in when the weather is too dreary for the great outdoors.

Founder and brewmaster Chad Ostram welcomes visitors with open arms and a full pint. He knows the drive makes it feel like you're in the middle of nowhere, so he makes it feel like home. And just in case you think good beer isn't enough reason to get there, he dazzles diners with award-winning barbecue from a truck and dinner specials from the kitchen.

He's gilding the lily. Ostram's sour beers are a happy surprise. **Thunderstruck** is a Scottish gruit (an ancient herb style of beer) aged in whiskey barrels with an 8 percent ABV. His **Jorge** is a pale ale made with jalapeños that he carried over from the previous owners. Rainy day? What rain?

Ostram was a software engineer and a home brewer for twenty years. He thought maybe in retirement he would do something like open a home brew shop. When the chance came up to buy Sweet Mullets, he jumped on it. He keeps between eleven and thirteen beers on tap and when old ones expire, he brings in new styles. You'll never be disappointed you made the trip!

THIRD SPACE BREWING CO.

1505 W. St. Paul Ave., Milwaukee, WI 53233; (414) 909-2337; thirdspacebrewing.com
Founded: 2016 **Founders:** Kevin Wright and Andrew Gehl **Brewer:** Kevin Wright **Flagship beers:** Happy Place Midwest Pale Ale, That's Gold! Golden Kolsch, Upward Spiral India Pale Ale, and Acres Edge Toasted Oatmeal Stout **Tours:** By appointment **Taproom hours:** Thurs, 4 to 9 p.m.; Fri, 2 to 10 p.m.; Sat, noon to 10 p.m.; Sun, noon to 5 p.m.

Good beer happens when a former biomedical engineer turned brewmaster fulfills a promise to a camp friend to start a brewery with him. Kevin Wright was the head brewer at Hangar 24 Craft Brewery in Redlands, California, but developed a hankering to return to his Wisconsin roots. Andrew Gehl was working as a corporate litigator in Chicago. They decided to return to Milwaukee, join in the brewery boom, and opened Third Space in the fall of 2016 in a former tin manufacturing space in Milwaukee's Menomonee Valley. They adopted the bones of the warehouse in the

UPWARD SPIRAL

Style: IPA

ABV: 6.50 percent

Availability: Year-round

Third Space brewer Kevin Wright spent years making beer in California, so he knows how to brew a true West Coast–style IPA. He just brews them in Wisconsin now. Upward Spiral is light on the malt bill, which lets the tangerine, pine, and grapefruit notes of the hops make that silky slide down the throat.

taproom—high ceilings and polished cement floor—but added long tables made from old machinery and tops coated and polished to a healthy shine. There are three levels of seating, including an outdoor patio with a sliver of skyline and colorful graffiti tagging on the building next door. Both kids and dogs are welcome here.

What sets Third Space apart is Wright's experience producing West Coast–style IPAs and his dedication to clean beers. Start with a **That's Gold Kolsch,** which is light but rich with taste. Maybe work your way to the **Upward Spiral,** a hoppy IPA with a smooth finish. Or, if you're hungry, start your trip across the road at Sobelman's, a place known for burgers and their outrageous Bloody Marys accessorized with a full fried chicken. Third Space's **Happy Place Pale Ale** is a pretty good chaser, because everyone knows that in Wisconsin all Bloody Marys are served with a beer chaser.

URBAN HARVEST BREWING

1024 S. 5th St., Milwaukee, WI 53204; urbanharvestbrewing.com/home

Founded: 2016 **Founders:** Steve Pribek and Mark Kaminski
Brewer: Steve Pribek **Flagship beer:** Corkscew, Espresso Amber, Nookie Nookie, Chinook Citra IPA **Taproom hours:** Wed and Thurs, 4 to 9 p.m.; Fri and Sat, 2 to 10 p.m.

Founders Steve Pribek and Mark Kaminski have fashioned a true urban taproom. There are three breweries on this stretch of 5th Street. Urban Harvest blends into its surroundings, closest to the Walker's Point neighborhood homes and its specialty Mexican restaurants.

Tables and chairs provide intimacy, but also allow patrons to see the brew works in the corner. Pribek left the vintage features, which matches the era of storefronts on the block, but updated it with a fresh look. And fresh beer. I'm a big fan of the **Urban Harvest Corkscrew IPA,** an IPA that is easy on the hops and won't make you thirst for water afterward.

Expect to see locals walking in with growlers to fill and sitting at the bar playing any of the games in a hall cabinet. Grab some popcorn or order something from the nearby Transfer Pizzeria or Milwaukee Tamale Co. Or stop in after shrimp soup from neighboring Botanas.

VENNTURE BREW COMPANY

facebook.com/VenntureBrewCo

Milwaukee border is in line for another brewery but this one combined with a coffee house. Photographers Simon McConico, Jake Rohde, and Rob Gustafson were still searching for funding and a building at deadline, but expect to open a coffee house and brewery, in 2017.

WESTALLION BREWING COMPANY

1825 S. 72nd St., West Allis, WI 53214; (414) 578-7998; facebook.com/stallionbrewing

Hours: Wed through Fri, 3 p.m. to 9 p.m.; Sat, noon to 9 p.m.; Sun, noon to 6 p.m.

Owners Erik and Kim Dorfner know beer. Kim is an event planner at Best Place at the Historic Pabst Brewery. Erik worked at Lakefront Brewery and is an avid home brewer. Westallion shares space with the landlord, but has the biggest slice for its brewhouse and taproom while the landlord has carved out a covered spot for his personal automotive repair center.

The brewery is off the Greenfield Avenue in West Allis, a main thoroughfare, but sits at the end of a tree-lined residential street. The signature beer will be a Vienna lager, but the brewery opened with a Hefeweizen and a Pilsner on tap.

While Milwaukee breweries were slow to join in the craft beer movement, its neighborhood bars were on it. These five are standouts in a city that embraces a well-made beer.

BRASS TAP

7808 W. Layton Ave., Greenfield, WI 53220; (414) 301-4054; brasstapbeerbar.com/greenfield

Open Mon through Thurs, 11 a.m. to 1 a.m.; Fri and Sat, 11 a.m. to 2 a.m.; Sun, 11 a.m. to 1 a.m.

The Florida chain arrived in the Milwaukee area around 2014. The bar has eighty taps and a selection of beers that will make your head spin. The Brass Tap hosts tap takeovers, a weekly Friday fish fry, and other local events.

BURNHEARTS

2599 S. Logan Ave., Milwaukee, WI 53207; (414) 294-0490; burnheartsbar.com

Open Mon through Fri, 3 p.m. to 2 a.m.; Sat and Sun, noon to 2 a.m.

You'll notice a theme in this Bay View neighborhood: it's chock full of top-flight beer bars. Burnhearts is in the thick of it. The beer list here is intense and the bartenders know what they're talking about. The bohemian hipster interior is welcoming. Burnhearts hosts an annual outdoor winter party each February called Mittenfest that draws thousands. I mentioned it was outdoors, right?

CHAMPPS AMERICANA

1240 S. Moorland Rd., Brookfield, WI 53005; (262) 797-6600

Open Mon through Thurs, 11 a.m. to midnight; Fri and Sat, 11 a.m. to 1 a.m.; Sun, 11 a.m. to 11 p.m.

The restaurant looks like a chain, thanks in part to its location next to a hotel and down the street from a mall. Don't be fooled, though. It's full of fresh beer. The staff takes field trips to breweries such as Lagunitas in Chicago or 3 Floyds in Munster to bring the good stuff home. Once or twice a year they break out the rare or cellared beers. They'll wait on you in record time, but be prepared for a crowd.

COMET CAFE

1947 N. Farwell Ave., Milwaukee, WI 53202; (414) 273-7677; thecometcafe.com

Open Mon through Thurs, 10 a.m. to 2 a.m.; Fri, 10 a.m. to 2:30 a.m.; Sat, 9 a.m. to 2:30 a.m.; Sun, 9 a.m. to 2 a.m. Food is only served until 10 p.m. every night.

Comet Cafe might not be the first place you think of when you think beer bar. If you're looking for a bacon bar, well, then Comet is your place. But the East Side cafe holds a series of beer schools worth your time and attention.

DRAFT AND VESSEL

4417 N. Oakland Ave., Shorewood, WI 53211; (414) 533-5599; draftandvessel.com/#home

Open Mon through Thur, 3 p.m. to midnight; Fri, 1 p.m. to 2 a.m.; Sat, 11 a.m. to 2 a.m.; Sun, 11 a.m. to 10 p.m.

An expansion took Draft and Vessel from cozy to more spread out, but the well-run beer bar didn't lose any of its charming intimacy in the process. The eighteen tap lines are a thing to behold, but the intimate nature of Draft and Vessel makes it impossible not to make friends with the beer lover next to you.

PALM TAVERN

2989 S. Kinnickinnic Ave., Milwaukee, WI 53207; (414) 744-0393

Open Mon through Sat, 5 p.m. to 2 a.m.; Sun, 7 p.m. to 2 a.m.

Don't let the dive bar exterior fool you. All dive bars should have this kind of rare beer collection or be able to mix cocktails with such, um, good spirits. Palm Tavern makes the list of *Draft* magazines best beer bars every year.

ROMANS' PUB

3475 S. Kinnickinnic Ave., Milwaukee, WI 53207; (414) 481-3396; romanspub.com

Open Tues through Fri, 5 p.m. to closing; Sat, 7 p.m. to closing.

You'll want to get to know Mike Romans, the proprietor of the establishment that bears his name. He saw craft beer coming and helped introduce it to Milwaukee. Check the website where he lists what's on tap, what's in cans and bottles, and what's next to be tapped. Servers are cicerone-trained. Mike also makes a delicious Manhattan. You'll learn all this if you're polite and don't ask for a Miller Lite.

THE SUGAR MAPLE

441 E. Lincoln Ave., Milwaukee, WI 53207; (414) 481-2393; mysugarmaple.com

Open Mon through Fri, 3 p.m. to closing; Sat and Sun, noon to closing

I have to say this was my first real "beer bar." On my visit, they brought out a list of beers from which to choose, but the staff guided, suggested, and talked me through the sixty craft beers on tap. Sugar Maple hosts special events such as beer school nights during which brewers talk about their product and offer beer samples that make you want to study harder.

WORLD OF BEER

418 N. Mayfair Rd., Wauwatosa, WI 53226; (262) 770-3902; worldofbeer.com/FindABeer/Wauwatosa

Open Mon through Thurs, 11 a.m. to 11 p.m.; Fri and Sat, 11 a.m. to 2 a.m.; Sun, 11 a.m. to 10 p.m.

Why yes, a Kolsch would taste delicious with southern fried pickles! Thanks for the suggestion, World of Beer. This chain opened in 2014. It offers hundreds of beers with about thirty on tap.

Appleton-Sheboygan-Oshkosh

Take the Lake Michigan Circle Tour highway to get here. It's pokier than the interstate, but it hugs the sandy beaches and breaking waves along the shoreline. Plus, there are ample opportunities along the way to tuck into town for a beer and a bite.

Magician Harry Houdini was born in nearby Appleton, and the History Museum at the Castle features stories about the famous escape artist among its exhibits. Appleton, in the heart of the Fox Valley, is close enough to Green Bay that teams competing with the Packers stay here. The Wisconsin Timber Rattlers, a minor league baseball team of the Milwaukee Brewers, also play here.

Go west and you'll discover distinct Wisconsin attractions, including the John Michael Kohler Art Center Sheboygan, which is known for its art collection as well as its concert series. Not so far away is the town of Kohler and the luxurious American Club, home to the sweeping landscape of the Whistling Straits Golf Course. The 2020 U.S. Ryder Cup is scheduled for the course.

You can visit most any time, but once a year people fly into the AirVenture Museum in Oshkosh to celebrate historic airplanes. We're looking at you, Harrison Ford. He attended the 2016 Fly In, sponsored by the Experimental Aircraft Association.

There are fifteen bike trails in the area if you want to see the city that way. Or hang out at the beach and watch surfers from a seat on the sand. Of course, there's a beer to go with any of these activities.

APPLETON BEER FACTORY

603 W. College Ave., Appleton, WI 54914; (920) 364-9931; appletonbeerfactory.com

Founded: 2013 **Founders:** Jeff Fogle and Ben Fogle **Flagship beers:** Bellwether Blonde American Ale, Butte des Morts Black, and Clock Out Oatmeal Stout **Taproom hours:** Tues, 4 to 10 p.m. or midnight; Wed through Sun, 11 a.m. to 9 p.m.

All aboard. It's a beer train.

Jeff Fogle, a tradesman pipe fitter, and his son, Ben, started the Appleton Beer Factory in a former auto parts store. The design is industrial, better to see the custom-fabricated beer train, a knee-high sized train that Fogle built, near the fermenters.

Work in the brewery was mostly done by hand and much of it by family members. It remains a family gig. Leah Fogle, Jeff's wife, is the chef; Mairi Fogle, Ben's wife, is the marketing manager.

You might think **The Butte des Morts Black,** a reference to a Wisconsin lake or maybe it's the unincorporated town, is a porter, but it's not—it has the body of a blonde. Ask about the beers, but also ask about the beer blends. The Hefeweizen combined with tequila and margarita mix becomes a **Heferita.** Beer flavors don't stop there. Here's your chance to try a hop-pickled egg.

P.S. *Butte des Morts* is thought to mean "hill of the dead."

BARE BONES BREWERY

4362 County Rd. S, Oshkosh, WI 54904; (920) 744-8045; barebonesbrewery.us

Founded: 2015 **Founders:** Dan Dringoli and Patti Dringoli. **Brewer:** R.J. Nordlund, brewmaster, and Jody Cleveland **Flagship beers:** Amber Ale and Dog Daze IPA. **Seasonal beer:** Harvest Ale **Taproom hours:** Wed and Thurs, 3 to 8 p.m.; Fri, 3 to 9 p.m.; Sat, noon to 9 p.m.; Sun, noon to 7 p.m.

You can see Bare Bones Brewery from the highway, look for the red corrugated metal building.

The name does double duty. It refers to Dan Dringoli's need to "keep it simple," and to the couple's love of dogs. They have rescued a few in their time, including the pit bull who serves as the brewery mascot. All dogs are welcome here. Dringoli said three or four come with their human counterparts regularly.

The couple built the bar at the edge of a golf course, and while it isn't the official nineteenth hole, it attracts a fair number of golfers discussing the game over a brew. You won't find televisions on the wall here.

Bare Bones is also on the Wiouwash Bike Trail, a 41-mile trail named for the counties—Winnebago, Outagamie, Waupaca, and Shawano—that it runs through. The brewery makes for a nice pit stop.

Brewmaster R.J. Nordlund makes a lot of one-off beers to serve a population that wants the next big thing. Be sure to ask about the **Chipotle Smoked Doppelbock.** While it's not always in stock, it's worth the question.

COURTHOUSE PUB

1001 S. 8th St., Manitowoc, WI 54220; (920) 686-1166; courthousepub.com
Founded: 2002 **Founder:** John Jagemann **Brewer:** Brian Sobel **Flagship beers:** Adam Street Ale and Munich Helles **Seasonal beer:** Imperial Butternut Ale **Taproom hours:** Mon through Sat, 11 a.m. to 9 p.m.

The Courthouse Pub is often a first stop for vacationers disembarking the *SS Badger*, the largest cross-lake passenger service on the Great Lakes and the only coal-fired steamship in operation in the U.S. *The Badger* ferries people and vehicles from Michigan to Manitowoc and back. The Courthouse Pub was once F. Dillinger's Beer Hall that became the Court Cafe during Prohibition. It had a few other lives, but seems to have settled into this one as a casual, sophisticated place for dining. There's a refined cocktail menu and a selection of brews from **Bavarian Weiss,** a non-filtered robot brew, to the **Dark Justice IPA,** a black IPA best served in a tulip glass. Also don't miss their seasonal **Imperial Butternut Ale,** made with caramelized butternut squash.

The microbrewery has a 4-barrel system, and space is at a premium, explains brewer Brian Sobel. That's why he brews with extracts instead of grain.

8TH STREET ALE HAUS

1132 N. 8th St., Sheboygan, WI 53081; (920) 208-7540; 8thstreetalehaus.com
Founded: 2010 **Founders:** Kurt Jensen and Randy Oskey **Brewer:** Eric Hansen **Flagship beers:** Freshwater Surfrider Kolsch, Hard Roll Hefe, and 30-Year-Old's Scotch Ale **Seasonal beer:** Autumn Moonbeam Amber **Taproom hours:** Mon through Thurs 4 p.m. to closing; Fri and Sun, 11 a.m. to closing

You can feel the Lake Michigan air on Sheboygan's 8th Street, and there's only one reason to go inside on a temperate afternoon—the food and beer at 8th Street Ale Haus.

Kurt Jensen and Randy Oskey created the beers crafted in the space next door, a former grocery store with a built-in smoker. Their expansion from 1-barrel system to a 10-barrel version means more **Greatest Love Machine** in bourbon barrels for you.

The **30-Year-Old's Scotch Ale,** which got its name because the brewer was thirty when he made it the for first time, is a lighter than average Scotch Ale. Have two.

The restaurant bustles, offering pages of entrees and appetizers, including vegan options—all that food and thirty-one taps of beer from which to choose a match. 8th Street Ale Haus keeps its own brews on tap as well as those from neighboring 3 Sheeps and other craft brewers, along with a selection of ciders. Jensen and Oskey helped create Sheboygan's Craft Cider Week.

If you stop in and unusual things are happening, it's likely one of two groups is in the house—Pints and Purls, a knitting and sewing group, or the Ale-Literate Book Club.

FOX RIVER BREWING

1501 Arboretum Dr., Oshkosh, WI 54901; (920) 232-2337 and 4301 W. Wisconsin Ave., Appleton, WI 54913; (920) 991-0000; foxriverbrewing.com
Founded: 1995 **Founders:** Jay Supple, Heidi Supple, John Supple, Joe Supple, and Doreen Supple **Brewer:** Kevin Bowen **Flagship beers:** Blu Bobber Raspberry Ale and Reel It In APA. **Taproom hours:** Mon through Thurs, 4 to 10 p.m.; Fri, 4 p.m. to closing; Sat and Sun: 11 a.m. to closing

Oshkosh is the flagship location Fox River Brewing. It's also the centerpiece. The family-run brewpub and restaurant sits on the edge of the Fox River and offers 200 outdoor seats, 30 dock parking spots, and an additional 200 indoor seats. Still need a chair? Head to the taproom. You can thank Seattle for what Jay Supple calls the best of both worlds. A few visits to the coastal city encouraged the family to develop a restaurant and brewpub on the water.

The brewery's proximity to the University of Wisconsin at Oshkosh—right next door—helps draw drinkers and diners. So does the popular **Blu Bobber Raspberry Ale.** A quick look on UnTapped offers the most back-handed but useful description of the brew: "I accidentally ordered a blueberry beer." He liked it.

Foods here are meant to be paired with beer, and a few are made with beer—such as the fish and chips, the beer cheeseburger, and the pretzel with beer sauce.

Supple is educated in Oshkosh beer history. Did you know the city's heritage includes Peoples Brewery, the first African-American–owned brewery in the U.S. in 1970?

KNUTH BREWING COMPANY

221 Watson St., Ripon, WI 54971; (920) 748-5188; knuthbrewingcompany.com
Founded: 2015 **Founders:** David Knuth and Marie Knuth **Flagship beers:** Blue-Eyed Blonde Farmhouse Ale, Workers Mild Brown Ale, and American Pale Ale. **Tours:** By request. **Taproom/restaurant hours:** Tues through Thurs, 11 a.m. to 9 p.m.; Fri and Sat, 11 a.m. to 10 p.m.

David Knuth's story is familiar. Someone gave him a home brew kit and he was off to the races. Only that someone was his father-in-law and the occasion was his bachelor party. The Ripon community thanks him.

Knuth spent several years in the restaurant business before he decided to open Knuth Brewing, a brewpub that offers craft beer and wood-fired pizzas. Knuth recently expanded operation and expects to brew 500 barrels a year.

Look up to see the tin ceilings and down to appreciate the hardwood floors. The front windows suggest a vintage storefront. The look appealed to Knuth and he wanted to keep as much of the original character as possible in the renovation. In its past life the building was a restaurant and bakery.

The menu reads more elegant than standard bar food. I don't know about you, but I'd order the salmon and a pint of the **Blue-Eyed Blonde**—named for Knuth's wife—for starters; the crisp blonde matches well with the salmon.

LION'S TAIL BREWING CO.

116 S. Commercial St., Neenah, WI 54956; (920) 843-3020; lionstailbrewing.com
Founded: 2015 **Founders:** Alex Wenzel and Kristin Wenzel **Brewer:** Alex Wenzel **Flagship beer:** Kula Wheat Golden Ale with Pineapple **Tours:** By appointment **Taproom hours:** Mon through Thurs, 3 to 10 p.m.; Fri, 3 to midnight; Sat, noon to midnight; Sun, 11 a.m. to 5 p.m.

The Lion's Tail tale begins with a Christmas gift that Alex Wenzel received, a home brewing kit that set the stage for a career switch from chemical engineering to brewery owner.

Wenzel didn't want to pick a flagship brew—the ale with pineapple is on tap all year—because he plans to roll out ten to fifteen beers each year. He has barrel-aged brews and sour beers to go with lagers and ale already in the rotation.

The brewery is located in a 109-year-old building that was once an insurance company headquarters. An old vault is reserved as an event space. The beer hall and game lounge are down a hallway. It's all charming high ceilings and wood trim.

And then there's this: A kind of choose-your-own adventure beer called the **Custom Pale Ale.** The Lion's Tail keeps a dozen French presses behind

KULA WHEAT GOLDEN ALE WITH PINEAPPLE

Style: Wheat beer
ABV: 5.6 percent
Availability: Year-round in the taproom and in a crowler
The flagship beer at the Lion's Tail Brewing Company is fermented with 125 fresh pineapples and Wisconsin-grown Tettnanger hops. The pour is golden and the finish is crisp.

the bar. Order it and they'll hand you a pint glass filled two-thirds of the way. You pick from one of ten hop varieties and drop hop in yourself using the French press. A timer is set for fifteen minutes. The customer gets to press the hops into the pint glass, then it's topped with cold, carbonated beer.

The Custom Pale Ale costs $12 but comes with a 10-ounce short pour of your choice to drink while you wait.

Lion's Tail doesn't serve food, but getting a pizza or some upscale pub food takes 10 minutes when you order from neighboring restaurants.

PLYMOUTH BREWING COMPANY

222 E. Mill St., Plymouth, WI 53073; (920) 400-1722; plymouthbrewingcompany.com

Founded: 2013 **Founders:** Joe Fillion and Nancy Fillion **Flagship beers:** Stafford Oatmeal Stout, Nutt Hill American Nut Brown Ale, Hubcity Hefeweizen, and The Mighty Mullett IPA **Brewer:** Joe Fillion **Tours:** By request. **Taproom hours:** Wed and Thurs, 5 to 10 p.m.; Fri and Sat, 5 to 11 p.m.

Joe and Nancy Fillion started Plymouth Brewing on a 1-barrel, 1-person system. One barrel for the beer, and convincing one person at a time in this city of 8,500 to give up his or her macro-beer for craft beer. With choices like their **American Nut Brown Ale** and its pistachio flavoring, who could resist? They did such a good job, they opened a production brewery across the street.

SILVER BLACK PHANTOM BIKE

Style: Imperial Milk Stout

ABV: 9.2 percent

Availability: Seasonal (usually autumn)

It's an accident that my favorite beers pack heat. The slight sweetness of the milk stout in Plymouth Brewing's Silver Black Phantom Bike sets the stage for the liberally applied chipotle and cayenne peppers available in autumn.

The taproom, like the brewery, is on Plymouth's main street. It's filled with pictures of Plymouth's history and beer memorabilia. You won't get much time to look at them, though. The conversation includes everyone. No wallflowers allowed.

Joe Fillion can't believe all small towns don't have a brewery. Neighbors fill up the place on weekends thanks to creative beers and friendly bartenders. He might be on to something. Why don't all small towns have a brewery?

ROWLAND'S CALUMET BREWERY

25 N. Madison St., Chilton, WI 53014; (920) 849-2534; rowlandsbrewery.com
Founded: 1990 **Founders:** Bob Rowland and Bonita Rowland **Brewer:** Patrick Rowland **Flagship beers:** Calumet Amber, Calumet Oktoberfest, Fat Man's Nut Brown Ale **Seasonal beer:** Calumet Wild Rice **Taproom hours:** Tues through Thurs, 2 p.m. to 2 a.m.; Fri and Sat, noon to 2:30 a.m.; Sun, noon to 2 a.m.

Not many breweries can boast a large operation malting company down the street. Rowland's can. In fact, the Rowland family can brag about a couple things.

Rowland's Calumet Brewery was the seventh biker bar—remember you're in the birthplace of Harley-Davidson—in the state and the fourth brewery in Wisconsin to serve beer on premises, said co-founder Bonita Rowland.

The brewery and the taproom, which is called the Roll In Brew Pub, is housed in what used to be Chilton's first fire station. After the brewery opened in 1990, the Rowlands answered a lot of questions about craft beer.

Rowland's sponsors an annual spring beer festival that draws up to 3,200 people. At least that's the number at which they cap the ticket sales. Now consider this: the population of Calumet hovers at 4,000.

The brewery began with a 3-barrel system and added a 7-barrel system that Bonita calls "Plant No. 2," in 2002.

Bob Rowland died in 2006. Son Patrick, who had been helping with the process, took over.

Rowland's is a classic Wisconsin bar. Pull up a bar stool, order a frozen pizza—they get them from Fond du Lac—and say "hi" to Bonita.

STONE CELLAR BREWPUB

1004 S. Olde Oneida St., Appleton, WI 54915; (920) 731-3322; stonecellarbrewpub.com
Founded: 2004 **Founders:** Steve Lonsway and Tom Lonsway
Brewers: Steve Lonsway (master brewer) and Craig Welch (head brewer).
Flagship beers: Scottish Ale and Vanishing Vanilla Stout **Seasonal beers:** Dopplebock, Blindsided Barley Wine, ESB, Blueberry Wheat, Dark Ale, Raspberry Porter, I.R.B.B.A.I.O.R.S., Stonetoberfest, Pumpkin Spice, 666, Grand Cru, and First Snow Ale **Tours:** By appointment as possible
Taproom hours: 11 a.m. to 10:30 p.m. (at least) daily.

Stone Cellar Brewpub is the oldest continually running brewpub in the state. It's also home to Stone Arch Brew House. Two names, one beer. Steve Lonsway explains that they started as Stone Cellar Brewpub and then got into bottling. The name became a trademark issue. The result? Stone Cellar mostly refers to the restaurant; the Stone Arch name represents the beers sold outside the restaurant.

At the stately brewpub, which does have a stone archway, you'll find beers in the English style, including the **English Six Grain Ale**, Tom Lonsway's "easy-drinking English ale with a complex malt profile and a nice hop balance." Open beamed ceilings and booth seating add to the European-style setting.

Steve Lonsway bounced through the beer industry, first as a home brewer then as owner of a home brew store before he and his father bought Stone Cellar. The building dates back to 1858 before a fire nearly leveled it. George Walter opened it in 1918, serving a popular Adler Brau beer. Fast forward to 2015, the Lonsways brew on a 7-barrel system, pumping out about 3,000 barrels a year.

Stone Arch uses a pilot brew system to expand selections. They've also brewed in collaborations with Biloba Brewing in Brookfield.

3 SHEEPS BREWING COMPANY

1837 North Ave., Sheboygan, WI 53083; (920) 395-3583; 3sheepsbrewing.com
Founded: 2011 **Founders:** Grant Pauly and James Owen
Brewmaster: Grant Pauly **Flagship beers:** Rebel Kent the First Belgian Style Amber Ale and Really Cool Waterslides India Pale Ale
Tours: Fri, 5 p.m. **Taproom hours:** Mon through Thurs, 4 to 10 p.m.; Fri, 3 to 11 p.m.; Sat, 11 a.m. to 11 p.m.; Sun, 11 a.m. to 7 p.m.

Silly name. Seriously good beer.

"Think three sheets to the wind," says Grant Pauly about how his brewery got its name.

Pauly was a home brewer before he made the leap to professional brewer after leaving the family concrete business. Smart move. Pauly and company give their beers whimsical names, but they're serious about taste. **Seven Legged Cartwheel** is an IPA fermented with *Brettanomyces bruxellensis Trois*. It adds tartness but doesn't cover hints of mango and pineapple.

HOPPY SPICE

Style: India Pale Ale

ABV: 11.20

Availability: Limited

This is a big beer. Giant even. Hoppy Spice, part of the 3 Sheeps' Nimble Lips Noble Tongue series, is made with earthy Chinook hops so you're getting the full flush of IPA bitterness along with the sock-in-the-face heat of ghost peppers. It's not an everyday beer. It's also not an everyday brewer who can add ghost peppers and not mask the taste of a well-brewed IPA.

In 2016, 3 Sheeps moved its taproom across town into a former Pepsi bottling complex. They turned the warehouse into the taproom with open garage doors that lead to an outside patio. Across the room, the size of half a football field, is the area where they hold the sour beers in barrels.

There's a story for everything from the tables to the wood railings, much of which were reclaimed from the city's former Armory. The fancy modern bathrooms are showcase level, what you might see at the nearby Kohler Company. But you're most interested in what's behind the bar, right?

The lush **Cashmere Hammer Rye on Nitro** comes in specially designed bottles, but try it here on tap. If it's a cool day, nuzzle and sip. That is autumn in a glass right there.

Pauly compares the taproom to Willy Wonka's Chocolate Factory because this is where visitors can try brews introduced only to Sheboygan County along with experimental beers.

They don't serve food, but food carts come by often. The Interurban Bike Trail stops close the taproom.

BRAVEHEART PUB

2120 Calumet Dr., Sheboygan, WI 53081; (920) 458-3231; braveheartpub.com
Open Tues through Sun, noon to closing

You could drink at many places in Sheboygan, but Braveheart's beer selection is amazing and constantly changing, as is the list of ongoing events. Be sure to check their website for the latest. **Narwhal Imperial Stout** on tap, anyone?

FOX RIVER HOUSE

211 S. Walnut St., Appleton, WI 54911; (920) 574-3950; facebook.com/Fox-River-House-93322479561/?fref=ts
Open Mon through Saturday, 3:30 p.m. to closing

What's not to love? The Fox River House has a long list of craft beers on tap and in bottles and cans—120 if you're counting. Enjoy them inside or with a concert on the expansive bier garden outside.

Madison

Saturdays in summer find Madison humming with hundreds of people carrying bags of vegetables. The state's largest farmers' market sets up outside the Capitol building turning the government center into a cornucopia of fresh crops, cheeses, and baked goods.

On Saturdays in autumn, the crowd gathers a little farther west at Camp Randall, where the University of Wisconsin Badgers play football and "jump around" is less a suggestion and more a requirement for anyone in the stands.

All of this is to suggest that Madison, a city with an isthmus sandwiched between Lake Monona and Lake Mendota, is a city of action as well as a seat of knowledge. It's also a place where craft beer rules and not just during the city's Beer Week each May.

Madison is the home of FEMS, Females Enjoying Microbrews, which started in 2012 out of Vintage Brewing. In 2015, the area's female brewers collaborated on the Common Thread brew made for Madison Beer Week. Ten brewers and other women gathered at Wisconsin Brewing to create a Belgian Tripel.

The Great Taste of the Midwest, one of the top beer festivals in the country and definitely in the Midwest, is organized by the Homebrewers and Tasters Guild.

Drink up. You're in the right place.

ALE ASYLUM

2002 Pankratz St., Madison, WI 53704; (608) 663-3926; aleasylum.com
Founded: 2006 **Founders:** Dean Coffey and Otto Dilba **Brewer:** Dean Coffey **Flagship beer:** Hopalicious American Pale Ale **Seasonal beer:** Tripel Nova **Tours:** Sun noon to 5 p.m. on the hour. Tickets go on sale starting at 11 a.m. at the brewery. **Taproom hours:** Sun, 11 a.m. to 10 p.m.; Mon through Thurs, 11 a.m. to midnight, and Fri and Sat, 11 a.m. until bar time.

Ale Asylum built the brewery in 2013 to specific standards. The bottling line is the same size as the former brewhouse. Co-founders Dean Coffey and Otto Dilba added dining rooms and two floors of outdoor seating.

The focus here is on beer. Diners can see the brewery from every room. There are no televisions in the building and that's intentional. Hathaway Dilba, one of the brewery owners, said a couple comes in each Friday. They take a seat in an alcove in the upstairs lounge and catch up with each other.

Ale Asylum holds the title as Madison's first microbrewery. They distribute in Wisconsin, Illinois, and, most recently, Minnesota.

VELVETEEN HABIT
Style: American IPA
ABV: 7.50 percent
Availability: Year-round
When Ale Asylum debuted **Velveteen Habit** in 2015, Wisconsinites declared it among the best IPAs nationally. And Wisconsinites are rarely wrong about beer. There's a floral note to the beer. Those are the hops getting your attention. But there's just enough softness to make you yearn for another. What palate fatigue?

Pull up a seat at the bar and enjoy the conversation with staff who seem to love what they're doing. They'll banter. They'll chat beers with you. They can tell you when to expect the next release of **Velveteen Habit,** an IPA that you'll crave ever after.

Other beers in the portfolio have names like **Bedlam,** a Belgian IPA, **Ambergeddon,** a West Coast–style amber, and **Sticky McDoogle,** a Scotch Ale. It's what you come to expect from a brewery named Asylum that refers to its fans as inmates.

There is a sense of whimsy in the taproom, too. Witness the cooler door marked only with Christopher Walken's photo. Think about it. You'll get it.

ALT BREW

1808 Wright St., Madison, WI 53704; (608) 352-3373; altbrew.com/home.html

Founded: 2012 **Founders:** Trevor Easton and Maureen Easton **Brewer:** Trevor Easton **Flagship beers:** Rustic Badger Farmhouse Ale and Hollywood Nights Blonde IPA. **Seasonal beers:** Pumpkin, Summer Solstice saison, and a bourbon barrel–aged brown. **Tours:** By appointment **Taproom hours:** Tues through Fri, 3 to 9 p.m.; Sat, 1 to 9 p.m.

Heads up when you walk in the taproom. Seriously. Look up. Above you is equal parts false ceiling and art project. Pieces of wood are artfully designed to suspend from the tall ceiling.

The ceiling isn't the only thing artfully created at Alt Brew. All their beers are gluten-free. And it started as an act of love.

COPPERHEAD

Style: Copper Ale

ABV: 5 percent

Availability: Year-round

Alt Brew's **Copperhead** won a silver medal at the 2016 Great American Beer Festival. Applause for gluten-free beers. Brewer Trevor Easton performs magic with sorghum, rice, honey, and millet to create a beer with hints of roasty chocolate.

Co-founder Maureen Easton has celiac disease. Wheat, barley, and rye make her ill. Home brewer Trevor wanted to create one beer she could drink and worked to create his gluten-free beers. When his friends couldn't tell his gluten-free brews from the ones with gluten, the couple opened the brewery and Alt Brew was born.

The space is small but uniquely designed with the taproom near the door. The other room leads to offices. There are two glass-walled views of the brewhouse. They sell crudités to go with the beers here. On the day we visited, a woman at the bar munches on carrots. One for her, one for the small dog at her feet. This is truly a unique space, so pull up a chair. Life's a pageant. Watch it with a beer in hand.

CAPITAL BREWERY

7734 Terrace Ave., Middleton, WI 53562; (608) 836-7100; capitalbrewery.com

Founded: 1986 **Founder:** Ed Janus **Brewer:** Ashley Kinart **Flagship beer:** Wisconsin Amber **Seasonal beers:** Maibock, Lake House, Oktoberfest, and Winter Skal **Tours:** Last 30 to 45 minutes. Tour times are listed on the website. Self-guided tours are available by request. **Taproom hours:** The Bier Garten is open Tues through Thurs, 4 to 9 p.m.; Fri, 3 to 10 p.m.; Sat, noon to 9 p.m.; Sun, noon to 5 p.m. April through October. The indoor Bier Stube is open the same hours November through April.

Capital is one of the oldest craft breweries in the state, and started brewing in the traditional German style. They continue that tradition with **Wisconsin Amber** and **Supper Club Lager.** Brewer Ashley Kinart created **Fishin' In the Dark,** an Imperial Schwarzbier, before being named head brewer. Since then she's helped bring **Grateful Red,** a red IPA, and others to the lineup.

This is old-school brewing. Well, it's an old-school brewery with long hallways and dark rooms, including the Bier Stube with its dark iron room dividers and Old World interior. If you're lucky when you visit, one of the owners will be behind the bar playing with new ways to present the beer. Maybe with a dusting of cinnamon sugar on the beer glass rim, which was the case when I visited.

The brewery sits at the edge of quaint Middleton, but quaintness gives way to a party atmosphere when the Bier Garten opens. A Friday night can bring as many as 1,500 people to Capital. There's a band shell to hold live bands and tables that can fill up quickly. Capital has its own bike club that meets twice a week. Visit capitalbikeclub.org for more information on that.

In the meantime, bring the family, bring the dog, bring some food. You can get the beer there.

CORNER PUB BREWERY

100 E. Main St., Reedsburg, WI 53959; (608) 524-8989; facebook.com/cornerpubbrews/
Founded: 1996 **Founder:** Pete Peterson **Brewer:** Pete Peterson **Flagship beers:** Porter and IPA **Seasonal beer:** Dill Pickle American Pale Ale **Taproom hours:** Mon through Thurs, 10:30 a.m. to 2 a.m.; Fri and Sat, 10:30 a.m. to 2:30 a.m.; Sun, 11:30 a.m. to 6:30 p.m.

For all of you who have walked into a diner and wanted a craft beer with your BLT, you've come to the right place. The Corner Pub Brewery calls itself the first brewpub in Reedsburg, which is funny if you consider that it's the *only* brewpub in the town of 9,000 residents.

The Corner Pub Brewery is known as the oldest operating tavern in Sauk County (although it hasn't always been the Corner Pub Brewery). It's also known for its **Dill Pickle American Pale Ale,** a challenging style that people seem to crave.

Time your visit for fall and Fermentation Fest (fermentationfest.com), an annual celebration of live culture in all its forms, from dance to yogurt, poetry to sauerkraut. The celebration includes farmers, chefs, artists, poets, and performers for nine days of tasting, demonstrations, classes, art events, and more throughout Sauk County.

GRAY BREWING CO.

2424 N. Court St., Janesville, WI 53548; (608) 752-3552; graybrewing.com
Founded: 1856 **Founders:** Joshua Gray (originally). Began brewing again under Bob Gray and Fred Gray. **Brewer:** Fred Gray **Flagship beer:** Honey Ale, Oatmeal Stout, Busted Knuckle Irish Style Ale, Bully Porter, British Style Brown Porter, Rock Hard Red carbonated, and Wisco Wheat. **Tours:** Sat, 1:30 p.m. **Taproom hours:** Fri, 5 to 7 p.m.; Sat, 12:30 to 4 p.m.

There are historic breweries in this guide. Gray's should be considered among them. Founded as a brewery and soda maker in 1856, Gray's stopped producing beer in 1912. They made mostly sodas until a 1992 fire destroyed the building. Rebuilding the brewery became an occasion to brew again. Gray's was back in the beer business in 1994 with **Honey Ale, Oatmeal Stout,** and **Wisco Wheat.** Gray's still makes classic soda styles and also an energy drink called Gray's Badger Blaster, available at Gray's Tied House.

The taproom is at the front of the tiny brewery on a busy road in Janesville. On my visit, the bartenders were pushing the **Rock Hard Red,** a malt beverage that goes down like a Gray's soda but packs a wallop. There's plenty of space in back for special outdoor events.

The brewery doesn't serve food.

GRAY'S TIED HOUSE

950 Kimball Lane, Verona, WI ; (608) 845-2337; graystiedhouseverona.com/home
Founded: 2006 **Brewer:** Fred Gray **Flagship beers:** Oatmeal Stout, Honey Ale, Wisco Wheat, Rathskeller Amber Ale, Busted Knuckle Irish Ale, and Rock Hard Red **Seasonal beer:** Bully Porter **Taproom hours:** 11 a.m. to 2 a.m., weekends, earlier on weeknights. The kitchen closes at 9 p.m. on weeknights and 10 p.m. on weekends.

Fred Gray opened Gray's Tied House in 2006 in Verona, about forty minutes from Gray's Brewing Co. in Janesville. The Tied House serves the same beer styles as the brewpub but also offers a full menu. You can think of it as a remote taproom with food named for an archaic business concept outlawed shortly after Prohibition. Before Prohibition, breweries would buy or finance bars in exchange for exclusive rights to serve their beer in that spot.

HOP HAUS BREWING COMPANY

231 S. Main St., Verona, WI 53593; (608) 497-3165; hophausbrewing.com
Founded: 2015 **Founders:** Phil Hoechst and Sara Hoechst **Brewer:** Phil Hoechst **Flagship beers:** Plaid Panther, Magic Dragon, El Andy, Jean Claude Van Dubbel, Peace Train, Wildcat Amber, and Super Big Time **Seasonal beers:** Fat Eddy, Hoppy Hour Hero, Notorious H.O.P. IPA, and a seasonal Belgian. **Tours:** By request **Taproom hours:** Mon through Thurs, 4 to 10 p.m.; Fri, 3 to 11 p.m.; Sat, noon to 11 p.m.

The outside of Hop Haus is deceptive. One might wonder, *Is it empty? It kind of looks empty.* It's not. The place hops, even though that's not what "hops" in the brewery name means. It means that the service is swift. That pizza you brought in with you will still be warm when you get your pint of **Jean Claude Van Dubbel.**

Phil Hoechst was a home brewer in Colorado a few years back when he and Sara moved back to their home state and her hometown. When they found the right space they opened Hop Haus as a tasting room and gathering place for the neighborhood and beyond.

Hop Haus serves pretzels, cheese curds, wings, and more, plus they allow patrons to bring their own food in. Board games are stacked on shelves in the hallway, but it's also easy to jump into conversation—especially if the University of Wisconsin Badger football game is on.

HOUSE OF BREWS

4539 Helgesen Dr., Madison WI 53718; (608) 347-7243; houseofbrewsmadison.com
Founded: 2011 **Founder:** Page Buchanan **Brewer:** Nick Kocis **Flagship beer:** Standing Stones Scotch Ale **Seasonal beer:** Russian Imperial Stout **Tours:** Leaves tours to HopHead Tour company. **Taproom hours:** Tues through Sat, 3:30 to 9:30 p.m.

House of Brews brewer Nick Kocis calls the area in which House of Brews is located "the Brewmuda triangle." That assertion is not without merit. Ale Asylum is 6 miles away and Next Door Brewing is 3 miles. But House of Brews's connection to craft brewing in Madison is nearly as easy to chart. Kocis brews his **Dead Bird** beer here, MobCraft brewed here for years before opening a brewery in Milwaukee in 2016, and the list goes on. Owner Page Buchanan is happy to brew for others. He gets paid up front and "it's a lot less stress" than wondering if he'll make his money back on sales.

Buchanan also hosts a CSB (Community Supported Brewery). Think vegetables and community-supported agriculture, but for beer. People join and receive a case of 22-ounce bottles each month.

It's worth the journey through the city to get to House of Brews. The small taproom isn't fancy, and beer is served in plastic cups from a cubby that looks more like a ticket booth than a bar, but the beer selection is strong and the beer is good. Plus, you'll get to try some experimental beers or others that have been tweaked.

DEAD BIRD BREWING

deadbirdbrewing.com
Founded: 2015 **Founders:** Nick Kocis, Jeremy Hach **Brewer:** Nick Kocis **Flagship beer:** Pamplemousse **Seasonal beers:** Strumpet, Strongman, Wine Thief, and Bourbon Vanilla Stout. **Tours:** If they're around **Taproom hours:** Each Sun at House of Brews is Dead Bird tap takeover day.

This isn't your typical brewing arrangement. Or is it? Nick Kocis is a brewer for House of Brews, a contract brewery. One of the breweries signed to brew at House of Brews is Kocis's Dead Bird Brewery.

Kocis explains: Dead Bird is paying House of Brews to manufacture the beer and the House of Brews is paying Kocis.

Yeah, well, it works. He gets to invent magical recipes like **Wine Thief,** a collaboration with the University of Wisconsin agriculture department and Cambridge winery. Kocis used 1,200 pounds of grape in the fermenter with his base beer. The result is a light, tropical, fruit-forward taste with gooseberry and mango notes.

Kocis and Hach were college roommates when they got the idea for Dead Bird. That's also when they named the brewery. The roommates found a huge old pot—the kind people in the '90s used to fry their Thanksgiving turkeys—in the attic at Hach's parents' house. They also found a dead sparrow at the bottom of it. Although it was scrubbed and sanitized to a tee, the two joked that every beer they made would have a dead bird in it. If you can't get past that, then you'll miss out.

KARBEN4 BREWING

3698 Kinsman Blvd., Madison, WI 53704; (608) 241-4812; karben4.com
Founded: 2012 **Founders:** Alex Evans, Zak Koga, and Ryan Koga **Brewer:** Ryan Koga **Flagship beers:** Fantasy Factory American IPA, Nightcall Smoked Porter, Tokyo Sauna American Pale Ale, Block Party American Amber Ale, Dragon Flute American Pale Ale **Tours:** Sat, 1 p.m. **Taproom hours:** Mon through Wed, 11 a.m. to 10 p.m.; Thurs through Sat, 11 a.m. to midnight, and Sun, 11 a.m. to 10 p.m.

Yup, you're in the right place. Looks like a store outside, right? Step inside. Relax. Order a **Lady Luck Irish Red** and some deviled eggs. Look at the artwork on the walls. Watch a brewer performing magic in the brewhouse in back. Order another beer. Try a **Fantasy Factory,** a light American IPA. You won't be able to tell from the pint glass but the bottle

FANTASY FACTORY

Style: IPA

ABV: 6 percent

Availability: Year-round on tap and in six-packs

I'll admit that the label with an armed cat on a unicorn and a rainbow caught my attention first. The balanced taste sucked me in. Karben4's **Fantasy Factory** has ready notes, probably from the English golden malted barley, but a citrus backbone that makes you want more.

label features a cat with a gun riding a unicorn. There's a rainbow involved.

This used to be where Ale Asylum brewed its beer but then the Karben4 founders took it over and made everyone forget they weren't the original brewers at this location. Another fun fact? All the meat served from the kitchen, excluding turkey, is fed with the mash from the brewery.

Karben4 is a small but mighty brewery and the beers are made in the English style. Malt bombs away. Grab a table and a board game inside or pull up a chair on the patio. I prefer the bar where you can watch the kitchen crew or chat up the bartenders who know all about the Karben4 beer styles.

Order another beer. Let the fantasy live on.

LAKE LOUIE

7556 Pine Rd., Arena, WI 53503; (608) 753-2675; lakelouie.com

Founded: 1999 **Founder:** Tom Porter **Brewer:** Tom Porter **Flagship beer:** Warped Speed Scotch Ale **Seasonal beer:** Louie's Reserve Scotch Ale **Tours:** One Sat a month at noon and 1:15 p.m. Check the website for dates.

Somewhere between Madison and Spring Green is Lake Louie Brewing. There's actually a lake there. Well, it's more like a pond that's named for Tom Porter's Uncle Louie, a teetotaler who used to own the property. Porter calls Lake Louie his midlife crisis brewery. After twenty years in the automobile engineering business, he cashed in his 401K and converted a metal storage shed into the start of a brewery.

Porter has made a go of it, that's for sure. His beers are sold around the state. Porter is his own best representative for the beer. Talk to any of the brewery owners in the Madison area and they'll testify that Porter helped them get started by answering questions, helping them understand equipment, and generally offering support. They share the story of how in the early days Porter would sleep next to the fermenter because it would quit in the middle of the night and he'd have to start it up again.

There's no taproom at Lake Louie, in fact he's not even open to the public except during the tours, which are held once a month. Check the website for tour dates and times. He does provide beer at the tours, and if you're lucky, you'll have a chance to sample Porter's **Warped Speed Scotch Ale,** a scotch ale brewed as it was in the 1700s. The brew has a light sweetness you expect from the style and a light hop finish. Classic. But since you're at Porter's place, you might also try the Tommy's Porter, a full-bodied porter that tastes of nuts and berries but has a coffee finish.

THE LONE GIRL

114 E. Main St., Suite 101, Waunakee, WI 53597; (608) 850-7175; thelonegirl.com

Founded: 2016 **Founders:** Kevin Abercrombie and Paul Kozlowski **Brewer:** John Russell **Flagship beers:** Speakeasy Ale, Off the Rails IPA, Sweet Stout, Right On! Rye, Pipe Dreams Wheat, Summer Lovin, and Barnwood Brown Ale **Taproom hours:** Tues, Wed, and Sun, 11 a.m. to midnight; Thurs through Sat, 11 a.m. to 2 a.m.

Your first stop at The Lone Girl should be the rooftop. Why? Because in Wisconsin, nice days aren't often wasted and The Lone Girl rooftop is a good place to appreciate them. There's also probably a band playing.

Kevin Abercrombie, who owns the restaurant Matilda in Chicago, moved to Waunakee five years ago. So it makes sense that he wanted to start something like The Lone Girl in Waunakee, a pretty community outside Madison. He had company, too. Octopi opened a few months ahead of The Lone Girl. What are the chances that a city of 13,000 would get two breweries in one year? But they have peacefully coexisted.

The Lone Girl combines a 10-barrel brewery with a brewpub atmosphere and a full-fledged restaurant menu. Families fill the place on weekends and you might have to wrestle a couple of adolescents for a spot at the bags games if it's late afternoon.

Grab lunch or dinner and definitely grab one of John Russell's brews. We suggest **Right On! Rye** for its earthy and spicy taste. It pours hazy and you'll get floral and fruity aromas. We bet you're going to want to take home a growler.

Brewing isn't Russell's only job. He's also an assistant scientist in the Division of Otolaryngology, Head and Neck Surgery at the UW-Madison School of Medicine.

According to Abercrombie, The Lone Girl name came from the fact that he and co-founder Paul Kizlowski have seven children between the two of them and only one daughter.

NEXT DOOR BREWING

2439 Atwood Ave., Madison, WI 53704; (608) 729-3683; nextdoorbrewing.com

Founded: 2013 **Founders:** Keith Symonds, Pepper Stebbins, Aric Dieter, and Crystal Dieter **Brewer:** Brian Krieter. **Flagship beer:** Bubbler Blonde Ale, Kaleidospoke American Pale Ale, and Plumptuous Scotch Ale **Seasonal beers:** Libations Saison and Motha Pucka Sour Blonde Ale. **Taproom hours:** Mon, 4 to 10 p.m.; Tues and Thurs, 11 a.m. to 11 p.m., Fri and Sat, 11 a.m. to midnight; Sun, 11 a.m. to 9 p.m.

The goal of Next Door Brewing is in the name. They want to be the neighborhood pub. So far, it's working for Madison's east side where the brewpub tucks neatly into a residential neighborhood. There's a Catholic church across the way and another brewery just up the street.

Inside, patrons choose from communal tables that seat twelve to fifteen people or sit at the bar where servers can advise on the best beer choice for the entree. Putting beer and food together is a focus for Next Door. There's spent grain in the beer pie, pale ale in the custard, and porter in the ganache.

Brewer Brian Krieter worked in nature conservancy and preserve management before he moved to Madison a few years ago at an ideal time to use his home brewing skills professionally. We recommend the **Plumptuous Scotch Ale,** Next Door's highest rated beer. It's a Scottish ale made with Bramling Cross hops that give it an additional flavor that blends with malts, adding plum and caramel notes.

PLUMPTUOUS SCOTCH ALE

Style: Scotch Ale/Wee Heavy

ABV: 9.5 percent

Availability: Year-round

Plumptuous became so popular that it's always available on tap. The Bramling Cross hops give it a flavor that blends with malts that add plum and caramel notes. I'm a sucker for a boozy Scottish ale and as a result I'm pretty picky about which ones I like. This one makes the list.

OCTOPI BREWING

111 Uniek Dr., Waunakee, WI 53597; (608) 620-4705; octopibrewing.com/welcome

Founded: 2015 **Founder:** Isaac Showaki **Brewers:** Team of four **Flagship beers:** Everything under the 3rd Sign Brewery label **Taproom hours:** Tues through Fri, 4 to 10 p.m.; Sat, 2 to 10 p.m.; Sun, noon to 7 p.m.

Credit Wisconsin's low beer tax rate for bringing Octopi Brewing to the state. Founder Isaac Showaki was a brewery consultant in Panama City and helped build a brewery in the Chicago suburbs before landing in Wisconsin. He met a family from Wisconsin on a walking tour of Paris who mentioned Waunakee. They're neighbors now.

Octopi is the contract brewer portion of the 3rd Sign Brewery. It provides the 50-barrel brewhouse and 100-barrel fermenters. A carbon filter water softener lets them replicate any water. Contracts come from breweries, startup breweries, and one hospitality chain. The facility can fill 35 kegs an hour and 150 bottles a minute.

Showaki wants to keep brewers acting as a team and won't name the four in charge, although each has a specialty in one part of the brewing process from beginning to barrel-aging.

The 3rd Sign name and philosophy was inspired by Gemini, the third sign of the Zodiac and the sign of twins. Beers are made in two styles to reflect that. For example: **Madagascar Vanilla Mild Ale** and **Sumatra Mild Ale** are two sides of one beer style. Equipment like a state-of-the art centrifuge and more lets brewers create dualities that stretch styles like **Columbian Kolsch** that bears the color of a traditional Kolsch but tastes of coffee. Take a minute. Wrap your head around that.

The taproom hosts bands on weekends and a taco truck parks outside Tuesday through Sunday when the weather allows. This is where the experimental beers are tested. On one day, the brewing team finished work and broke out some barrel-aged favorites.

People getting off the interstate and those who work in the industrial park where Octopi lives, stop in after work to take home a crowler.

ONE BARREL BREWING

2001 Atwood Ave., Madison, WI 53704; (608) 630-9286; onebarrelbrewing.com
Founded: 2012 **Founder:** Peter Gentry **Brewer:** Peter Gentry **Flagship beers:** Commuter Kolsch, Penguin Pale Ale, and Banjo-Cat Black IPA. **Taproom hours:** Mon through Wed, 4 to 11 p.m.; Thurs and Fri, 4 p.m. to 1 a.m.; Sat, noon to 1 a.m.; Sun, noon to 11 p.m.

Peter Gentry combines DIY and family. The one-time home brewer included his dad when he opened his corner brewery. Well, he included his dad's skill. The elder Gentry helped renovate the place. In fact, he built the bar you'll sit at. Peter builds the beers.

Flights are available so we tried one. We picked well. The **Penguin Pale Ale** poured more copper than I would expect, but a quick sniff located tangerine and grapefruit. **Banjo Cat** pours dark like a stout, but the dry hop addition in the brewing process claims the beer's title as a Black IPA. Breakfast beer **Imperial Coffee Stout**, has the unexpected taste of butterscotch. Just a little.

Gentry named the brewery One Barrel because he literally brews one barrel at a time, which means inventory changes often. Customers are welcome to view each aspect of the brewing process from nearly any seat in the house.

If you leave One Barrel to head to Next Door Brewing (or vice versa), be sure to stop by Gail Ambrosius Chocolatier (2086 Atwood Ave). It's no coincidence that her staff can recommend chocolates that match well with beer.

PARCHED EAGLE

5440 Willow Rd., #112, Westport, WI 53597; (608) 204-9192;
Founded: 2012 **Founders:** Jim Goronson and Tom Christie **Brewer:** Jim Goronson **Flagship beer:** Hop-Bearer, Crane Ale, Parched Eagle Golden Ale, Janethan, Verily **Seasonal beers:** Decembeufest, Chingada Caca, Westportierfest **Taproom hours:** Wed and Thurs, 3 to 11 p.m.; Fri, 3 to midnight; Sat, noon to midnight

Parched Eagle nanobrewery will remind you of any of Wisconsin's neighborhood bars. The difference is that they don't serve spirits and they make fine beer. Well, Jim Goronson makes fine beer.

Goronson trained at the Siebel Institute and worked with Page Buchanan, owner of Madison's House of Brews. That's also where Goronson, who is

typically behind the bar slinging his own beers, makes them. He also brews at the taproom, but the House of Brews in Madison brews batches of the **Kolsch** and **Crane Ale.**

Parched Eagle serves pizzas, pretzels, cheese, and sausage. They also serve up jokes. Note the old pianos. Goronson insists the instruments make Parched Eagle "Westport's piano bar."

Wash down a pizza—once you smell one cooking you won't be able to resist—with a **Hop-Bearer,** where three hops added in eight different steps help make the American-style IPA a match for cheese and sausage. Want to go in a different direction? Try **Verily,** a Belgian Trappist Dubbel with a ruby red color and slightly sweet taste.

PORT HURON BREWING CO.

805 Business Park Rd., Wisconsin Dells, WI 53965; (608) 253-0340; porthuronbeer.com

Founded: 2012 **Founders:** Tanner Brethorst and family **Brewer:** Tanner Brethorst **Flagship beers:** Honey Blonde, Amber Alt, Hefeweizen, Porter **Seasonal beers:** Oatmeal Stout, Oktoberfest, Million Dollar Smoked Maibock (in collaboration with Madison's One Barrel Brewing) **Taproom hours:** Fri, 3 to 9 p.m.; Sat, 2 to 9 p.m.; extended hours in summer.

This has to be the first brewery named for a steam engine, a 1917 Port Huron steam traction engine owned by the Brethorst family since the 1950s to be exact. It still runs and the family shows it at the annual Badger Steam & Gas Engine Club Steam Show.

When he's not operating his steam engine, brewer Tanner Brethorst is creating beer. Something he's been doing since the age of twenty-one. While in college, he landed an internship at Tyranena Brewing Company in Lake Mills. From there he attended the Siebel Institute and studied in Germany. He worked at both Lake Louie and Capital Brewing before striking out on his own.

You can sample his beers in the Port Huron's taproom with its twelve bar stools and long tables in the beer hall style that encourages visitors to talk to each other. The picture windows overlook the 17-barrel brewhouse and allow patrons to watch the magic happen.

ROCKHOUND BREWING CO.

4445 S. Park St., Madison, WI; (608) 285-9023; rockhoundbrewing.com
Founded: 2016 **Founder:** Nate Warnke **Brewer:** Nate Warnke **Flagship beer:** Mosquito Bite IPA. **Seasonal beer:** Bock and Farmhouse ale. **Tours:** By appointment **Taproom hours:** Mon through Thurs, 11 a.m. to 11 p.m.; Fri and Sat, 11 a.m. to 1 a.m.; Sun, 9:30 a.m. to 11 p.m.

On our visit to Rockhound Brewing Company we witnessed an interesting sight. On one side of the bar, a group of four men were trying to engage a group of women who were celebrating a bachelorette party. If it weren't for the beer, this might not have ended well.

And yet, it did.

Founder and brewer Nate Warnke had just this in mind when he opened Rockhound after a dozen years in the corporate world. He wanted a comfortable setting and good balanced beer.

The Rockhound name comes from Warnke's stint as a geology major at the University of Wisconsin at Madison. He carries the rock theme throughout. For example, there is the blonde **Sandstrone** ale, a light and moderately hopped session; the **Shot Rock,** a Scotch ale aged on charred oak; and the **Balanced Rock Rye,** a well balanced American rye named for the rock formation at Devil's Lake State Park. There are others. Be sure to check them all out and, ahem, rock on.

TYRANENA BREWING CO.

1025 Owen St., Lake Mills, WI 53551; (920) 648-8699; tyranena.com

Founded: 1999 **Founder:** Rob Larson **Brewer:** Rob Larson **Flagship beers:** Three Beaches Honey Blonde, Headless Man Amber Ale, Rocky's Revenge American Brown Ale, Chief Blackhawk Porter, and Down 'n Dirty Oatmeal Stout **Seasonal beers:** Barred-aged Rocky's Revenge and Brewers Gone Wild **Tours:** Sat, 2 and 3:30 p.m. **Taproom hours:** Mon through Thurs, 4:30 to 10 p.m.; Fri, 3 to 11 p.m.; Sat, 3 p.m. to midnight; Sun, noon to 8 p.m.

Tyranena is in the land between Madison and Milwaukee, which puts it in a world of its own. The legend they like to tell is that a foreign tribe built stone structures and effigy mounds on the edge of a lake they called Tyranena, hence the name.

When you enter the brewery and taproom at the edge of a business plaza, the dogs will probably be the first things you see; Cal and Tucker run the place. They could show you around, but the brewery is small enough to be self-explanatory. Straight ahead is the brewery and to the right is the dark taproom. Teachers gather here at the end of a rough day, and on summer weekends, locals grab picnic blankets, gather dogs and kids, and head here to listen to bands or enjoy a wood-fired pizza, depending on which food truck is on the grounds.

Stacey Schraufnagel, who heads operations in the front of the building, thinks the brewery can feel like an extension of the living room for patrons. Rob Larson thinks "it's the beer."

BALLING THE QUEEN

Style: American Double/Imperial IPA

ABV: 9 percent

Availability: Rotating, part of the Brewers Gone Wild! series

I'm not a fan of honey in real life. In beer life, honey is the glue to the citrus and tropical flavors from Magnum, Cascade, Citra, and Simcoe hops. **Balling the Queen** is a medium-bodied beer that stings like a delicious bee.

Schraufnagel coordinates the brewery's community events, which include a bike ride, a run, a dog wash, and beer in the park during the summer. You don't want to miss selections from the **Brewers Gone Wild** series when they are offered. They are part of a series of "big, bold, ballsy beers." Some get re-released and some never come back. Get them while you can.

If you go for the tour, here's a silly fact: The bright tanks are named for Larson's female friends and exes.

One more tip: Call ahead if you want to bring Fido. Staff will tell you if the crowd is too big or just right for your dog to visit.

VIKING BREWPUB

211 E. Main St., Stoughton, WI 53589; (608) 719-5041; facebook.com/Viking-Brewpub-287023058126682/

Founded: 2014 **Founders:** Vik Malling and Lori Malling **Brewer:** David Worth **Flagship beers:** Soot in My Eye black IPA, Nordic Blonde light lager, and Midnite Sun cream ale. **Seasonal beers:** Big Stout schwarzbier and Xmas Ale Dopplebock **Tasting room/restaurant hours:** Mon, Wed, and Thurs, 4 to 11 p.m.; Fri, 4 to midnight; Sat, 11 a.m. to midnight; Sun, 11 a.m. to 8 p.m.

You have to see the dragon smoke. Co-founder Lori Malling's brother, Mitch Brickson, built the centerpiece of Viking Brewpub—a dragon head at the end of the bar. And it smokes. A click of a button and vapor comes out of the dragon's mouth.

That's not the only reason to visit, of course. There are the beers. **Soot in My Eye** is an inspired name for a smooth IPA. **Sjokglade Porter**—which translates to chocolate porter in English — is both spot on and a nod to the city's Nordic roots, which are visible from the architecture to the holidays celebrated. Try the meatballs, too. Vik Malling says they can't make enough of them.

Vik spent twenty-five years in the U.S. Air Force before putting down roots in Stoughton. He and his father-in-law would take regular trips to brewpubs for craft beer. When the opportunity came up to start his own, he and Lori went for it.

They stayed true to the style of this city of 13,000 residents. Stoughton celebrates two big events each year—Syttende Mai, a Norwegian Constitution Holiday celebrated for three days each May, and the Stoughton Coffee Break Festival. Stoughton is the birthplace of the coffee break and the city celebrates all things coffee each August.

WOODSHED ALE HOUSE

101 Jackson St., Sauk City, WI 53583; facebook.com/WoodshedAleHouse/

Founded: 2010 **Founders:** Brittany Kraemer, Trent Kraemer, Mark Kraemer, Scott Manning, Bryan Manning, and Mike Bridges **Brewers:** Scott Manning along with Dave Dewayne and Joe Virnich **Flagship beers:** Weissnix, Woodshed IPA, Scaredy Cat, and McLovin Irish **Seasonal beers:** Hibiscus saison, Jinja Ninja, Honey cream, Oktoberfest, Better Off Red, and Pumpkin Disorderly **Tours:** By appointment **Taproom/restaurant hours:** 11 a.m. to bar time, daily

It's handy to have a brewer in the family when you want to start a brewpub. Scott Manning was brewing in Arizona when his hometown, and most of his extended family, beckoned. The result is the original Vintage bar in Madison, Vintage the brewpub, and Woodshed Ale House in Sauk City.

Manning has won awards for his **Woodshed IPA,** a beer he originally imagined making the trip from England to India as an IPA. But he added modern touches, splitting the hop varieties equally between American and English hops and then brewing it with French oak chips, creating the current concoction.

The beers here have creative names. The chef has a creative touch. And the bar restaurant is decorated in an eclectic style. Sit in the leather couches or get a table by the window overlooking the brewery. Enjoy the black and white poster-size images of celebrities.

Vintage brews all its beers at the Madison site and they are also available at Vintage Spirits and Grill (529 University Ave.) in Madison.

WISCONSIN BREWING

1079 American Way, Verona, WI 53593; (608) 848-1079; wisconsinbrewingcompany.com

Founded: 2013 **Founders:** Carl Nolen, Mark Nolen, Kirby Nelson, and Mike McGuire **Brewmaster:** Kirby Nelson **Flagship beers:** Golden Amber Lager, Yankee Buzzard IPA, Chocolate Lab porter, Ol' Reliable Helles Lager, Psychops Intense Pale Ale, Inaugural Red, and Nectarine **Tours:** Reserve online, walk-ins welcome. **Taproom hours:** Tues through Thurs, 3 to 9 p.m., Fri, 1 to 11 p.m., Sat, 11 a.m. to 11 p.m., Sun, 11 a.m. to 8 p.m.

Tucked away in an industrial park with patriotic street names, the modern $11 million Wisconsin Brewing building defies the uniformity of a warehouse location.

The patio wraps around the steel and glass front of the building to the side overlooking a pond. Adirondack chairs feature backs carved into the shape of the state of Wisconsin so you know where you are.

Another clue to your location comes from the **Inaugural Red** on tap, the lager-style red with hints of tobacco was the first in a collaboration between the brewery and the University of Wisconsin-Madison. The partnership helped create the Campus Craft Brewery.

The 80-barrel brewhouse inside is another site to behold. Co-founder Kirby Nelson commands it from a keyboard in a small room inside. He's the master behind the **Golden Amber Lager** and the reason that Iowa's Toppling Goliath, stretched to capacity, decided to contract brew here for a while.

The over-the-top capacity allows the brewery to work with those specialty products while continuing to brew its own lineup. Nelson was behind **Josephine,** a spiced espresso beer and has future plans for a double bock, a Pilsner, and possibly a gueuze.

"What Wisconsin makes makes Wisconsin" is the theme here. "We take our name very seriously," Nelson said. It's one of the reasons the brewery decided to produce **Nectarine,** an 1800s recipe from vintage Madison brewery Fauerbach. The beer's history suggests it was a hop and malt tonic that was once available in pharmacies.

But they don't take themselves all that seriously. They know how to have fun. On weekends, you're likely to find a yoga class or an '80s night celebration at the brewery. One night they found a guy passed out under the fermenter. Don't worry, though, they learned their lesson. They barricade things now.

Nelson calls beer an adjunct to the quality of life. Well, that and pups. He brings his daschunds in on Fridays and Saturdays. The rest of the time, Mike McGuire's Irish Setters—flown in from Ireland—have the run of the place.

WISCONSIN DELLS BREWING CO.

110 Wisconsin Dells Pkwy., Wisconsin Dells, WI 53965; (608) 254-5337; dellsbrewing.com

Founded: 2002 **Founders:** Mark Schmitz, Jack Waterman, Turk Waterman **Brewer:** Jamie Baertsch **Flagship beers:** Rustic Red, Honey Ale, Kilburn Hop **Seasonal beers:** Strawberry Lemonade, Pumpkin Ale, Milk Stout, Stand Rock Bock **Tours:** By appointment **Hours:** Open 11 a.m. to 11 p.m. for food and beer

Jamie Baertsch almost always has an audience as she works from the open-air brewery. Her work day begins at 6 a.m., but tourists who visit the Dells to take advantage of the water parks and other amusements can see Baertsch work up to 3 p.m. Wisconsin Dells Brewing is located inside Moosejaw Pizza where diners can watch Baertsch and staff brewing, canning, and bottling from nearly anywhere in the dining room. They are part of the family fun vibe of the restaurant. Baertsch calls it "approachable." The kids can have a soda made on premises and make a Moosejaw hat while they chow.

Baertsch calls her beers approachable, too. For those who aren't beer geeks or think they don't like beer, the brewer recommends the raspberry beer. For the beer geeks, there are some barrel-aged beauties to try.

Crowds are seasonal in the Wisconsin Dells, but the beer is all year-round.

BRASSERIE V

1923 Monroe St., Madison, WI 53711; (608) 255-8500; brasseriev.com

Open Mon through Thurs, 11 a.m. to 11 p.m.; Fri and Sat, 11 a.m. to midnight; Sun, 4 to 11 p.m.

Brasserie V wants you to believe they are little bit of Belgium in the state's capital. Seeing is believing. They have 26 rotating taps and 300 bottles of European beers.

HOPCAT

222 W. Gorham St., Madison, WI; (608) 807-1361; hopcat.com/madison

Open Mon through Thurs, 11 a.m. to midnight; Fri and Sat, 11 a.m. to 2 a.m.; Sun, 10 a.m. to midnight

The Michigan-based craft beer bar carves out a section of 30 draft lines for local Wisconsin beers. Impressive gift, Michigan.

THE OLD FASHIONED

23 N. Pinckney St., Madison, WI 53703; (608) 310-4545; theoldfashioned.com

Open Mon through Fri, 7:30 a.m. to 2 a.m.; Sat, 9 a.m. to 2 a.m.; Sun, 9 a.m. to 10 p.m.

More than one Madison brewer credited their time behind the bar at The Old Fashioned for inspiring a career in making beer. The Old Fashioned's retro-theme and homage to all things Wisconsin makes it a popular stop.

SHOWBOAT SALOON

24 Broadway, Wisconsin Dells, WI 53965;
showboatsaloon.com (608) 253-2628.
Open Sun through Thurs, 11 a.m. to 2 a.m.; Fri and Sat, 11 a.m. to 2:30 a.m.

Sometimes when you're in the middle of a tourist location that aims at families and bachelorette parties, you want a choice of beers to drink. Showboat Saloon has you covered. Choose from their twenty-four beers on tap.

Lake Geneva-Whitewater

Lake Geneva was a summer retreat created for and by Chicago's barons of industry in the 1800s. The Wrigley mansion still stands and when it rains, it pours on the former home of the family who created Morton's Salt. The nearby rich and famous used the beaches as their playground. The first Playboy resort was built here in 1968. It closed in 1981 and was replaced by a resort and spa.

Lake Geneva has retained a sense of being set apart. It's Wisconsin, but not quite. It's not Chicago, but it can look like it with all the Cubs and Bears apparel.

In summer, take a boat excursion and see mansions from the water. For 101 years, the US Postal Service has delivered mail by boat to up to seventy residents on Lake Geneva. The Mail Boat Tour lets visitors come along.

Yerkes Observatory is open year-round. There's a zip line. Each year Lake Geneva hosts a winter fest in tandem with a national snow sculpting competition.

Whitewater—less than 30 miles away—is home to the University of Wisconsin-Whitewater and a variety of outdoor adventure options such as biking or fishing on Whitewater Lake for Largemouth Bass, Northern Pike, and Walleye.

841 BREWHOUSE

841 E. Milwaukee St., Whitewater, WI 53190; (262) 473-8000; 841brewhouse.com

Founded: Became 841 Brewhouse in 2015 **Founders:** Jim Burns and Lucas Burns **Brewer:** Mark Strehlow **Flagship beers:** Oatmeal Stout, Warhawks Wheat, 841 Amber, and 841 IPA **Taproom hours:** Daily, 10:30 a.m. to midnight (restaurant closes earlier)

Craft beer in a college town? Of course. **Warhawk Wheat** is named for the UW-Whitewater's athletics teams. Apparently they are pretty good. Fall temperatures call for the **Oatmeal Stout,** but when the game is on and the weather is nice, you'll support the team and your taste buds with **Warhawk Wheat.**

Alongside broasted chicken, 841 serves up **Oatmeal Stout.** Wing Wednesday calls for an **841 Amber** to extinguish the flame. You get the idea. The beer goes with the food.

The brewery is visible from the dining area, but you can also see the four taps featuring the beer made on premise. Eight taps are devoted to other brews.

GENEVA LAKE BREWING CO.

750 Veterans Pkwy., Lake Geneva, WI 53147; (262) 248-2539; genevalakebrewingcompany.com

Founded: 2011 **Founder:** Pat McIntosh **Brewer:** Pat McIntosh **Flagship beer:** No Wake IPA. **Seasonal beer:** Imperial Cherry Stout **Tours:** By request **Taproom hours:** Sun and Mon, 11 a.m. to 3 p.m.; Wed and Thurs, 3 to 7 p.m.; Fri and Sat, 11 a.m. to 8 p.m.

Pat McIntosh was retired when he went to business school and then opened the brewery close enough to a Home Depot to make local residents' long visits to the hardware store suspicious.

The brewery and taproom are tucked in the back of an office park that looks shuttered on weekends. Not so for the brewery, where you will find people playing cards, drinking beer, and swapping stories.

"It's totally different than a bar," McIntosh said. The taproom is small. Conversation is a choice but so is listening in. While we were there, we overheard the bartender sharing tales of Chicago with a customer while a couple and their son talked about their travels with a stranger.

Kegs block the aisle and the tanks are in full view. Yup, it's a brewery. Many of the beers are lighter and don't hit an ABV of 7 percent. But when they do, hoo ha. The **Implosion Double IPA,** for example, comes in at 9.30 percent ABV.

That will set you up for a day at the beach.

SECOND SALEM BREWING COMPANY

111 W. Whitewater St., Whitewater, WI 53190; (262) 473-2920

Founded: 2014 **Founders:** Christ G. Christon and Thayer Coburn **Brewer:** Christ G. Christon **Flagship beer:** Beast of Bray Road Amber Ale **Seasonal beer:** Wild Mane of LaGrange Hefeweizen **Tours:** By request **Taproom hours:** Mon through Fri, 11 a.m. to closing; Sat and Sun, 10 a.m. to closing

Talking about this brewery is a history lesson in Whitewater. The beers are named for local legends. For example, the **Beast of Bray Road,** which won a medal at the World Beer Cup in 2016 pours reddish-copper in color then surprises with a pine finish. The ABV of 6.66 is intentional, part of the mythology of the namesake, a werewolf creature reportedly sighted

BEAST OF BRAY ROAD

Style: American Amber

ABV: 6.66 percent

Availability: Year-round in bottles and cans

I guess a 7-foot-tall creature of the woods would smell a little like herbs. **Beast of Bray Road** has notes of spice, herbs, and just a little pine. Appreciate the effort it took to get to 6.66 percent ABV. This American amber ale drinks easy and pairs well with just about anything.

in nearby Elkhorn in the 1990s. **Witchtower Pale Ale** is named for the water tower in nearby Starlin Park, so called because residents believed that witches gathered at the stone tower to perform ceremonies and rituals going back to the beginning of the twentieth century. Whitewater was known as Second Salem because of its reputation as a place for witch gatherings.

Even if none of these stories were true, they are good stories. Co-founders Christ G. Christson and Thayer Coburn thought so, too, and recreated them on the Second Salem beer bottle labels.

Christon has his own interesting story. He's a second generation immigrant who worked in his family's restaurant from the moment he could walk. Christon then bought the building his father owned for two decades. The brewpub came later. "I was thirty years old," said Christon, "and Whitewater had NASCAR or college bars. I was trying to create a place I would go to with my wife." He succeeded.

And he continues to. A win at the Madison beer and cheese fest with **Bone Orchard IPA** made him confident enough to enter the World Beer Cup.

Enjoy a **Beast of Bray Road** on the patio with a lake view. Don't even think about the spooky history.

THE BOTTLE SHOP

617 W. Main St., Lake Geneva, WI 53417; (262) 348-9463; thebottleshoplakegeneva.com

Open Sun through Tues, 11 a.m. to 6 p.m.; Wed and Thurs, 11 a.m. to 7 p.m., Fri and Sat, 11 a.m. to 8 p.m. Wine tastings are offered on Sat, 1 to 4 p.m.

Technically, this isn't a beer bar. It's a liquor store with a great beer selection. And you're allowed to open the beer on premises. The Bottle Shop is probably more well known for its wine selection, but the beer inventory is getting there. Grab a fresh baguette and cheese at the store and a spot on the sofa for the live entertainment and special events.

Southwest

Southwest Wisconsin cuts a broad swath from the western edge of the state known as the Driftless to farmland hills winding just beyond the state's capital in Madison. Follow the Mississippi River south from LaCrosse or head east to Spring Green and the prairies that inspired Frank Lloyd Wright to build his home Taliesen. See world-class Shakespeare performed at American Players Theater. Take your time cutting through small towns. Meet the residents. They're the reason beer has a following here.

Learn about history and eat award-winning cheese in Mineral Point. Feel like you're in Switzerland in New Glarus where telltale blue and white flags fly proudly. Grab a meal at the Glarner Stube which serves Swiss favorites like Wiener Schnitzel and Kalberwurst.

Take a side trip to Gravity Hill in Shullsburg and experience a wonder of physics. On Judgement Road (all the streets have Bible-inspired names) near County Road U, park your car on the road, put it in neutral, then take your foot off the accelerator and brake. The car appears to back up, uphill, for half a mile.

There's an emerging concentration of hop growers in this area who are once again taking advantage of the rich soil just as their predecessors did a century ago when Sauk County produced one-fifth of the world's hops. Wisconsin's craft beer movement is helping feed this resurgence. As you travel the curvy roads, keep your eyes open for ribbons of hops fixed to wires and tethered by telephone poles.

BREWERY CREEK INN

23 Commerce St., Mineral Point, WI 53565; (608) 987-3298; brewerycreek.com
Founded: 1998 **Founders:** Jeff Donaghue and Deb Donaghue **Brewer:** Jeff Donaghue **Flagship beers:** Jeff Donaghue prefers to think of beers in terms of light, dark, and in between. **Tours:** By request **Taproom hours:** Nov through May: Tues through Thurs, 11:30 a.m. to 8 p.m.; Fri and Sat, 11:30 a.m. to 8:30 p.m. June through Oct: Tues through Sat, 11:30 a.m. to 8 p.m.; Sun, 11:30 a.m. to 3 p.m.

Halfway between Madison, Wisconsin and Dubuque, Iowa is the town of Mineral Point, a sleepy community save for the Shake Rag Alley arts retreat, Pendarvis historical site, and the community's affinity for repurposing and reclaiming products, buildings, and history.

In 1829, Mineral Point was bustling with lead and zinc miners. It had a population larger than Chicago or Milwaukee and while not quite so many people live there anymore, the ones who do have turned it into a pleasant stop for travelers. One such stop is the Brewery Creek Inn, an 1854 stone warehouse that Jeff and Deb Donaghue renovated into a smart and cozy bed and breakfast with a bonus 15-barrel brewery on site. Jeff, a longtime home brewer, started out brewing antique beer styles such as an **18th Century Porter,** but he discovered that his customers would often ask for a pale ale. Jeff still brews his favorites, but surrounds them with ones the public craves such as **Brewery Creek Pale Ale.** Get a lesson in international beer drinking from Jeff, too. He explains his pale ale is what Americans call it. In England, the same beer is a bitter when it's on draught, but a pale ale in the bottle. At Mineral Point, it's a smooth pale ale either way.

The restaurant and inn have a symbiotic relationship, working together to become a destination for those planning a weekend getaway.

DRIFTLESS BREWING

102 Sunbeam Blvd., Soldiers Grove, WI 54655; (608) 624-5577; facebook.com/DriftlessBrewingCompany
Founded: 2013 **Founders:** Christopher Balistreri, Cynthia Olmstead, Michael Varnes-Epstein, and Scott Noe **Flagship beers:** Kick-Axe

LOCAL BUZZ HONEY ALE

Style: Wheat Ale

ABV: 4.8 percent

Availability: Year-round

The honey used to make Driftless Brewing's Local Buzz Honey Ale is so local it has the same zip code. The ale is golden light in color and tastes more of caramel and honey than it does wheat.

Pale Ale and Local Buzz Golden Ale **Tours:** Yes, call ahead **Taproom hours:** Open hours vary, but growlers are filled Thurs and Fri, 1 to 6 p.m.

Grab a beer, Driftless has a story you should hear. It began 12,000 years ago when retreating glaciers skipped over the land leaving behind picturesque bluffs, rivers, and grassland well-suited to farming.

The people who live here respect that simple stroke of luck. They believed in green, sustainable living before sustainable was cool. But they were also thirsty.

Four friends got together to start Driftless Brewing by deconstructing a solar-powered grocery store. The plan was to become a destination brewery for the fishermen, bicyclists, and fellow nature lovers who pass through. It is a work in progress. They're still working on the taproom, but the beer, well, they've got that down.

Driftless sources ingredients "as close to the brewery as we can," says co-founder Michael Varnes-Epstein. The honey in the **Local Buzz,** for example, is from a farm down the road from the brewery. The fresh honey adds color and natural hint of sweetness to the golden ale. The group of founders not only talk-the-talk—they walk-the-walk, as well. One lives off the grid and another trucks water to the brewery from a well on his sustainable farm. They chose beer names that are as down to earth (pun intended) as they are.

Sip a Dirt Brown Ale, a malty brown ale with hints of chocolate and a malt backbone. Order a **Solar Town Stout** and ask about the name. You'll get a glimpse into the town's history.

While they're getting the taproom off the ground, two of the four founders have day jobs, so it's wise to call ahead to see when the brewery might be open. Or knock. They'll accept a knock. Visitors get a tour, samples, and often cheese and crackers. The cheese is really good in these parts. You can also time a visit for the Driftless Art Fest, always the third Saturday in September. You won't see the brewery, but you'll be able to try the beer in the park just steps away.

FOUNTAIN CITY/ MONARCH PUBLIC HOUSE

19 N. Main St., Fountain City, WI 54629; (608) 687-4231; monarchtavern.com
Founded: 1997 **Founders:** John Harrington and Lori Harrington
Brewer: Contract brewed **Flagship beers:** Fountain Brew, Prairie Moon Red Lager, Eagle Valley Harvest Gold Pilsner, Irish Valley Spring Bock, and John Robert Porter Oatmeal Coffee Porter **Taproom hours:** Mon, noon to 9 p.m.; Wed and Thurs, 5 to 9 p.m.; Fri, noon to 10 p.m.; Sat and Sun, 11 a.m. to 10 p.m.

Fountain Brewing made beer from 1856 to 1965 before going out of business. But Fountain Brewing's former assistant brewer Wilbert Schmitt retained the purchasing and brewing records, which made it possible to bring back pre-Prohibition recipes from the taps at the Monarch Public House.

Co-founder John Harrington hopes to build a brewery between the Monarch Public House and adjoining property and use the basement as a taproom (it's already a small bar) and a gift shop.

In the meantime, he has the old recipes brewed elsewhere and brought to the Monarch Public House. They're on tap at the Irish-themed restaurant

ready to fill pint glasses and growlers. Harrington's constant companion is a rescue pup named Keeva Cara, but she's rarely lonely. All dogs are welcome.

HOP GARDEN TAPROOM

Behind the Old Mill, 6868 Canal St., Paoli, WI 53508; (608) 848-7666; thehopgarden.net
Founded: 2015 **Founders:** Rich Joseph and Michele Joseph
Flagship beers: Farmstead Ale, Nuggetopia IPA, and Festiv Ale
Seasonal beers: Pumpkin **Tours:** Growing season tours of the nearby hop farm are available by reservation **Taproom hours:** Wed and Thurs, 4 to 8 p.m.; Fri, 1 to 8 p.m.; Sat and Sun, 11 a.m. to 8 p.m.

Sneeze and you might miss the town of Paoli. It would be your loss. Nestled at the edge of the Sugar River and surrounded by the Paoli Mill Terrace and Park, the scenery couldn't get much better, unless, of course, you're viewing it from the Hop Garden Taproom.

Hop Garden beers are brewed not so far away at Madison's House of Brews. Co-founder Rich Joseph trucks the kegs to the taproom much the same way he trucks the hops from his farm to House of Brews for the brewing process.

Joseph grew up on farms, so it wasn't a stretch to start his own hop farm. But it wasn't a snap, either. He helped start the Wisconsin Hop Exchange cooperative. During Hop Exchange sales calls he talked with other brewers about his home-brews and they encouraged him to make his beer public.

Joseph likes the convenience of having someone else brew his recipes and having a taproom near the farm. Experience has taught him what kind of impact hops can have in a recipe, what the flavors mean, and how to build on that. "That terroir thing with grapes, we feel that's the case with hops as well," he said.

Johnson's **Festiv Ale** session brew draws cyclists from the Sugar River Trail. It has more than enough flavor to quench a thirst, but a low enough ABV for more biking. The Sugar River Trail meanders to at least one other brewery. His seasonal **Pumpkin,** made with pumpkins grown on the family farm, satisfies in the fall.

HILLSBORO BREWING CO.

815 Water Ave., Hillsboro, WI 54634; (608) 489-7486; hillsborobrewingcompany.com
Founded: 2012 **Founders:** Kim Verbsky and Snapper Verbsky
Brewer: David Bietz **Flagship beer:** Joe Beer and Bohemian Club Pilsner **Taproom/restaurant:** Tues through Sun, 11 a.m. to 10 p.m.

Kim Verbsky and Snapper Verbsky are busy people. Snapper, his given name, has a construction company and they are raising a family. So no big deal to start a pizzeria and brewery, right? What started as a pizzeria in Hillsboro evolved into a brewery for Snapper's dad, Joe, to test his skills as a home brewer.

Kim and Snapper had just opened the restaurant when Joe died unexpectedly. His porter recipe, named **Joe,** lives on and according to Snapper has become the most popular beer for locals.

Veteran brewer David Bietz is in charge of brewery operations, including the production center a couple blocks away from the pub.

"I'm more of a tank scrub who writes the checks," Snapper said.

Beers are distributed north to LaCrosse and south to Madison. Outside Hillsboro, **Bohemian Club Pilsner** is the most popular. Except for Baraboo, where the **Irish as Feck Irish Red Ale** is beloved.

The pub is working on more crossover between food and beer. Brisket has long been simmered in brew but cooks are now playing with ways to put spent grain in the pizza crusts.

"We're a small brewery and we're always going to be a small brewery," Snapper said. He credits his wife with the original credo: "Do a few things and do them well."

GRUMPY TROLL

105 S. 2nd St., Mount Horeb, WI 53572; (608) 437-2739; thegrumpytroll.com
Founded: 1998 **Founders:** Jack Slocum and Annette Slocum
Brewer: Mark Knoebl **Flagship beers:** Hoppa Loppa IPA, Captain Fred Lager, Eric the Red Amber, Sunflower Farmhouse Ale, Spetsnaz Stout, Maggie Imperial IPA, Monk Golden Ale, and Dragon Ship Wit.
Tours: Dates are listed in advance on the website. **Taproom hours:** Daily, 11 a.m. to 9 p.m.

The city of Mount Horeb banked its future on trolls. Trolls of varying degrees of trollness are hidden in plain sight in the city. One of them can be spotted at Grumpy Troll. A former creamery and cheese company, Grumpy Troll now pumps out beer and pizzas to the community. Belly up to the bar and you might find yourself chatting with strangers. Maybe you'll meet, as we did, a couple of retired men from Chicago hoping to visit every brewery in Wisconsin and taking notes on the flight in front of them. Or a guy who loves the drive because his motorcycle—a Wisconsin-made Harley-Davidson, perhaps—hugs every twist and turn of the rural countryside. Nah. They're here for the beer.

The flagships are almost always on tap, but **Thirsty Troll** is likely to offer seasonal delights as well. A bourbon barrel-aged in winter or a summer hefeweizen.

Work off the calories with a walk through the quaint downtown. Grab a sheet from the visitors' center and see if you can find all nineteen trolls, which are both a nod to the nearby historic Blue Mounds and a play on the divergent ethnicities—German, Irish, and Norwegian—who settled in Mount Horeb.

MINHAS CRAFT BREWERY

1208 14th Ave., Monroe, WI 53566; (608) 325-3191; minhasbrewery.com/minhas-craft-brewery-wisconsin
Founded: 1845 **Current owners:** Ravinder Minhas and Manjit Minhas **Flagship beers:** Lazy Mutt Farmhouse Ale, Huber Bock, 1845 Pils, and Swiss Amber. **Tours:** Mon, 11 a.m.; Tues through Thurs, 1 p.m.; Fri, 1 and 3 p.m.; Sat, 11 a.m., 1, and 3 p.m.; Sun, 1 and 3 p.m. **Taproom hours:** Daily 8 a.m. to 5 p.m.

Minhas is one of the oldest breweries in Wisconsin and in America. The former Joseph Huber Brewing Co. has changed hands in that time (winning Chicago Bears coach Mike Ditka can brag about being a one-time owner on his resume). Brother and sister Ravinder and Manjit resurrected the brewery's popularity with tours and contract brewing for forty businesses from Trader Joe's to Costco. They also opened a distillery directly across the street in the small town of Monroe—a town known for being the only place in America that produces the stinky but savory Limburger cheese.

Tours of Minhas start in the Lazy Mutt taproom with a free beer. They cross the street to the packaging facility where the line can fill 550 cans a minute. Same for the bottling line next to it. Brewers work two ten-hour shifts to brew from 12:01 a.m. to 10 p.m. The packaging line starts at 5:30 a.m. Minhas delivers to Guam, Costa Rica, Honduras, China, and Canada, where the Minhas family is from.

Tour guides give the checkered brewery history and visitors leave with samples to sip there and more to take home. Stick with the **Lazy Mutt IPA** with its spice and citrus tones and **Huber Bock** with its dark brown color and light coffee taste.

Stay after the tour to meander through the Herb and Helen Haydock World of Beer Memorabilia Museum. The couple's collection of lithographs and other breweriana has been valued at more than $1 million.

Also check the taproom for more details on stories you'll hear on the tour. They include tales of smuggling beer to Chicago speakeasies in milk cans and a kidnapping by Al Capone's associates that ended with then brewery owners, the Blumer family, refusing to pay the ransom.

NEW GLARUS BREWING

2400 State Hwy. 64, New Glarus, WI 53574; (608) 527-5850; newglarusbrewing.com

Founded: 1993 **Founders:** Deb Carey and Dan Carey **Master Brewer:** Dan Carey **Flagship beer:** Spotted Cow, Moon Man, Scream IPA, Serendipity, Champ du Blanc **Seasonal beers:** Uff-Da Bock, Staghorn Octoberfest and Bubbler hefeweiss **Tours:** Self-guided tours are Mon through Sat, 10 a.m. to 5 p.m.; Sun, noon to 5 p.m. Hard Hat Tours are Fri, 1 p.m. (3 hours long, begin at the original Riverside Brewery and end at Hilltop) **Taproom hours:** Mon through Sa, 10 a.m. to 5 p.m.; Sun, noon to 5 p.m.

New Glarus Brewing repeatedly makes the Brewers Association list of the Top 50 breweries in the U.S. based on beer sales volume. They were number 20 in 2015. But, here's the kicker: New Glarus brews are sold only in Wisconsin. That tells you something about the quality of the beer.

This is also a love story. The couple moved to Deb's home state and sold their house in Colorado to buy brewing equipment that would become New Glarus Brewing. It's a story Deb tells best, but a documentary called *Tale of the Spotted Cow* also features the couple's love story with each other, beer, and the community whose name they adopted for their brewery. The movie is a play on the name of the brewery's wildly popular **Spotted Cow,** a farmhouse ale that has been suggested as a gateway for macro-beer lovers who want to try a craft beer. In 2016, New Glarus added **Spotted Cow Grand Cru,** a bolder version of the original.

After building a new, state-of-the art Hilltop Brewery, the Careys repurposed the original Riverside Brewery for Dan's wild fruit caves. Switching over meant adding a koelschip and moving the bottling line to make room for award-winning sours, lambics, and Research and Development beers that are available only at the brewery and only four times a year (an online calendar gives the release dates).

New Glarus the village pays homage to all things Swiss. New Glarus the brewery is the castle on the hill with a grand staircase and vista views. Regular tours are held at the Hilltop Brewery, where visitors can stroll past polished copper kettles and watch through Plexiglas windows as brewers make the beer. You'll note that the hoses are waist height. Deb Carey made the ergonomic change because it was better for employees. The next step was to make the brewery employee–owned.

If it's spring or summer, head outside to the ornate patio. Follow a path to a spot where the view of farmlands makes it easy to understand why the

UFF-DA

Style: Wisconsin Bock

ABV: 7.3 percent

Availability: Seasonal

There are tastes of chocolate and coffee but New Glarus Brewing's **Uff-da** isn't nearly as sweet as it sounds. This was a tough choice. I love all the Research and Development beers New Glarus makes, but because New Glarus is only sold in Wisconsin, I didn't want to make it twice as frustrating for those out-of-state. **Uff-da** is a solid go-to beer in fall.

Swiss settled here, or stay close to the beer and enjoy some food from a local food truck.

Beer brought you here. You might bring beer home. Hilltop also has a beer depot on the lower level for retail sales of **Moon Man** pale ale, fruit beers, and, of course, **Spotted Cow.** For fun, count the out-of-state license plates in the parking lot. Nearly 5,000 people visit on weekends.

PEARL STREET BREWING

1401 St. Andrew St., LaCrosse, WI 54603; (608) 784-4832; pearlstreetbrewery.com

Founded: 1999 **Founders:** Tony and Joe Katchever and Tami Plourde **Brewer:** Joe Katchever **Flagship beers:** DTB Brown Ale and Linalool IPA **Tours:** Fri, 5 and 6 p.m.; Sat on the hour 1 to 4 p.m. **Taproom hours:** Tues through Thurs, 4 to 8 p.m.; Fri, 3 to 10 p.m.; Sat, noon to 7 p.m.

Pearl Street Brewing was on Pearl Street when it opened, that's how it got its name. It's also why people call at least once a week to ask if the brewery is on Pearl Street. It's not. In 2003, it moved to St. Andrew Street to a multi-story building that used to be a footwear factory. The bar that holds the pints? They built that from scratch. The pretzels everyone raves about? Not homemade, but they taste pretty good with a **Rubber Mills Pilsner,** a classic German-style pilsner that is clear straw yellow in color and has the slightest scent of lemon. Oh yeah, before they made footwear here, it was a rubber mill.

The scene here is informal. There is likely someone playing pool or ping pong or foosball. A family of four might borrow one of the board games from the bookshelf. Mostly people come here for beer. Flights are popular and include seven varieties of beer. You pick, but I suggest a **Me, Myself and IPA,** a logical choice for all seasons, or the seasonal **Linalool,** which is made with a wild Wisconsin hop more than twice the amount of linalool, a prized aromatic compound that gives hops their essence.

The microbrewery is on track to produce 7,000 barrels, about twice what it did the year before. Don't believe me? Ask Isa, the brewhouse dog. Employees bring their dogs, too. If we're being honest, so do customers.

Pearl Street also has live music every Friday night.

POTOSI BREWING

209 S. Main St., Potosi, WI 53820; (608) 763-4002; potosibrewery.com

Founded: Originally in 1852; revived in 2008 **Founders:** The Village of Potosi **Brewer:** Steve McCoy **Flagship beers:** Good Old Potosi, Cave Ale Amber Ale, Snake Hollow IPA, Czech Style Pilsner, and Potosi Light **Specialties:** Steamboat Lemon Shandy **Tours:** Fri, 6 p.m.; Sat, 12:30, 2, and 3:30 p.m.; Sun, 12:30 and 2 p.m.; or by request **Taproom hours:** Daily, 10:30 a.m. to 9 p.m.

Potosi Brewing gives you three reasons to stop in: the brewery, of course; the taproom, which serves a mean hamburger; and the **Good Old Potosi,** a blonde ale that will go great with that burger. Okay, four reasons if you count the silo-sized funnel-top Potosi beer can across the street.

There's also an adjacent museum called the Great River Road Interpretive Center and Transportation Museum, which tells the story of life on the Mississippi byway, and the National Brewery Museum and Library, which chose this town of 700 residents over larger municipalities like St. Louis to host its permanent display of breweriana.

Potosi is about beer, but it's also about community spirit. The brewery, once the fifth largest in the state, helped support families in town until 1972 when it shut its doors. In 2001 the building, which takes up much of the city's Main Street, was donated by its owners to the Potosi Foundation and the brewery re-opened in 2008.

The revived Potosi building includes pieces of the old brewery, the taproom, a patio large enough for live music, the museums, and event spaces. Look into the cave from the museum's lobby or take a peek at it through Plexiglas windows as you walk into the taproom.

Across the street is the new state-of-the art brewery. The Foundation is the sole owner and all profits are used to support historical and educational initiatives and other charitable causes.

SKELETON CREW BREW

570 Theater Rd., Suite 100, Onalaska, WI 54650; (715) 570-9463; skeletoncrewbrew.com

Founded: 2016 **Founders:** Todd Wiedenhaft and Jennifer Wiedenhaft **Brewers:** Todd Wiedenhaft and Jennifer Wiedenhaft **Flagship beers:** Arrr Ale American Pale Ale, Red Beard Irish Red Ale, Abandon Ship IPA, Hempen Halter Honey Nut Brown Ale, Pillage and Plunder Black Porter, and Shiver Me Timbers Oatmeal Stout **Seasonal beers:** Powder Monkey Red Ale and Hefeweizen Pumpkin Spice **Taproom hours:** Wed through Thurs, 4 to 9 p.m.; Fri and Sat, noon to 9 p.m.; Sun, noon to 5 p.m.

Todd and Jennifer Wiedenhaft received their first fermentation kit as a Christmas gift from relatives who own a vineyard in Minnesota. They made a lot of wine in the next seven years, Todd said.

Then they opened Lost Island Wine. A brewery was always part of the plan and the couple opened Skeleton Crew Brew in mid-2016 in the same building. The tasting room offers both wine and beer. They also have a home brew store in the same location. Like the **Honey Nut Brown Ale?** They'll show you how to make it.

Lost Island Wine has a Caribbean theme that the couple continued throughout Skeleton Crew Brew—bright colors, a tiki hut, a waterfall, and reggae and beach music serenading customers.

Todd is used to brewcationers stopping in. He gets referrals from nearby breweries and refers patrons to others as well. He and Jennifer also help arrange brewery and wine tours by bus.

TURTLE STACK BREWERY

125 2nd St., LaCrosse, WI 54601; (608) 519-2284; turtlestackbrewery.com

Founded: 2015 **Founders:** Brent Martinson **Brewer:** Brent Martinson **Taproom hours:** Wed and Thurs, 4 to 9 p.m.; Fri, 4 to 11 p.m.; Sat, noon to 11 p.m.; Sun, noon to 4 p.m.

Founder and brewer Brent Martinson was in medical school and working on a Ph.D., but brewing was his creative outlet. He can multitask with the best of them, which works well in his current job.

Nestled by the LaCrosse Center Arena, a parcel of new hotels, and a breeze of a walk to the Mississippi River, Martinson's brewery seats about fifty people comfortably and has already become a favorite spot for some

GERMAN PILS

Style: German Pils

ABV: 5.3 percent

Availability: Year-round

This is the style that will tell you if they're doing it right. They're doing it right at Turtle Stack Brewery. The grains in their **German Pils** provide the right sweetness and though I generally like a bolder beer, this is a good low-ABV alternative.

of the city's academics. And while it took some work to get the brewery in shape—the least of which involved peeling up several layers of flooring to find the aged hardwood floor underneath—the design came together. That's reclaimed barn wood on the tables and the polished bar top.

Martinson works on a 3-barrel system but uses 4 to 6 barrels for fermentation. That allows him the flexibility of an always rotating selection of brews. He's forever working with recipes, tinkering here or there to get the taste he wants. Half his job is education.

Now about that name. It references the Mississippi River where turtles are known to climb on each other trying to get the best sun. But there's another reference, too. It pays homage to a popular children's book that depicts a turtle king increasing the size of his kingdom by stacking his turtles to create a taller throne. One turtle has the courage to disrupt the throne, free the turtles in the stack, and send the once powerful king into the mud. It signifies the power of the individual.

TWO BEAGLES BREWPUB

910 2nd Ave. N., Onalaska, WI 54650; (608) 519-1921; twobeaglesbrewpub.com
Founded: 2016 **Founders:** Steve Peters and Christie Peters **Brewer:** Steve Peters **Flagship beers:** Amber, Kolsch, Milk Stout, and Pale Ale **Seasonal beer:** Sour Cherry Wheat **Taproom hours:** Mon through Fri, 3 to 11 p.m.; Sat and Sun, 11 a.m. to 10 p.m. Kitchen closes earlier.

Steve Peters was a home brewer in the 1990s. He went pro working for contract brewer City Brewing in LaCrosse. Now he has his own brewpub.

A chef takes care of the kitchen; Peters is in charge of the brews. You can watch him in the brewhouse through the glass, if you can tear your eyes away from the incredible views of Lake Onalaska.

Five of the eight taps at Two Beagles come straight from the bright tank. Other beers are rotated in and out. Peters plays with styles and names. The **Smokin' Larry** is a rauchbier spinofff of **Larry,** a kolsch-style brew named for Peter's friend who likes, "just plain, yellow beer."

BAUMGARTNER'S

1023 16th Ave., Monroe, WI 53566; (608) 325-6157; baumgartnercheese.com

Sun through Thurs, 8 a.m. to 11 p.m.; Fri and Sat, 8 a.m. to midnight

Here's where I admit that my family has been coming here for decades. The eclectic bar, cheese, sandwich, and chili restaurant anchors a charming square in downtown Monroe, walking distance from the Minhas Brewery.

Order a cheese sandwich—Limburger, if you dare—and then choose a Wisconsin craft beer or a legit German beer from the twenty-four tap lines. Give the wait staff a dollar and they'll perform a feat of physics by wrapping the bill just so, attaching a thumb tack and sending it soaring to the ceiling. The bills are collected twice a year for charity.

Central

Journey through Central Wisconsin where bodies of water sport evocative names such as the Tomorrow River or the Rat River. In between, right around Waupaca, is the Chain of Lakes, a connection of twenty-two lakes, which could mean twenty-two times the boating fun.

Wisconsin isn't a one-season state. Rib Mountain State Park, whose peak is visible from the highway outside Wausau, draws downhill skiers who want to take advantage of the natural snow cover.

Don't discount the miles of farmland and small towns as boring. You would miss some unexpected gems. For example, the village of Rosholt, population 500, hosts an annual bluegrass festival each August.

Whatever brings you to the area, don't forget the brew.

BLUE HERON BREWPUB

108 W. 9th St., Marshfield, WI 54449; (715) 389-1868; blueheronbrewpub.com

Founded: 2005 **Founders:** Paul Meier, Rita Meier, Tom Hinke, and Paula Hinke **Brewer:** Ron Hulka **Flagship beers:** Honey Blonde Cream/Blonde Ale Hybrid, Tiger's Eye English Mild Ale, and Hope Heart IPA **Seasonal beer:** Southbound Chili Rye Ale **Taproom hours:** Daily, 11 a.m. to close

You definitely won't go hungry at the Blue Heron Brewpub. Or thirsty. Enjoy pub food downstairs or go upstairs where they've added the Oven Above the Pub, a wood-fired oven for pizzas and flatbreads. Your choice.

Same with the beer styles. There is a mountain of seasonal brews from which to choose, but the flagships will also work some magic while you learn the history of Parkin Place, a Marshfield landmark. For those who want something light, the **English Mild Ale Tiger's Eye** will fit the bill with its low 3.7 percent ABV. At the other end of the spectrum is the **Anniversary Belgian Strong Ale** with tastes of honey, raisin, and caramel along with a hefty 9.2 percent ABV.

If you're smart, you'll plan your visit around the Blue Heron's Oktoberfest celebration. Specialty beers, live music, and proceeds for charity keep things hopping.

BULL FALLS BREWERY

901 E. Thomas St., Wausau, WI 54403; (715) 842-2337; bullfallsbrewery.com

Founded: 2007 **Founders:** Mike Zamzo and Don Zamzo **Brewer:** Mike Zamzo **Flagship beer:** Five Star Ale **Seasonal beers:** Bock Lager, Bourbon Barrel-Aged Oatmeal Stout, Uber Nacht Dunkelweizen Doppelbock, and Oktoberfest **Tours:** 1:30 p.m. Saturday and by appointment. **Taproom hours:** Mon through Thurs, 4 to 11 p.m.; Fri and Sat, 1 p.m. to 12 a.m.; and Sun, 11 a.m. to 7 p.m.

The parking lot here is usually jammed thanks to the live music offered. On our visit, a country band plays under a big white tent set up for the season. Under the big top, there is beer for the thirsty, gyros from a food truck for the hungry, and long tables set up for conversation. Live concerts are frequent events at the brewery. But the taproom regularly fills up with locals who come in for a six-pack or a growler fill.

FIVE STAR ALE

Style: Amber Ale

ABV: 6.1 percent

Availability: Year round

Bulls Falls Brewery's **Five Star Ale,** named in honor of the brewmaster Mike Zamzo's five daughters, has warming red tones. You'll smell fruit, but the taste comes from Golding hops. There's a sweetness that doesn't overwhelm the warmth of the beer.

Beers are steeped in German heritage, which explains the many lagers. Bull Falls would seem to be the last brewery to offer an IPA, but they do. The **Hop Worthy IPA** is made with Wisconsin-grown hops, but true to Bull Falls style, has a malty backbone. Bull Falls connects with the neighborhood with a selection of beers steeped in the German style and its ability to build community around it.

The story of Bull Falls (a territory at one time), Wausau, and its early settlers is reflected in framed stories on the wall. Look closely and you'll find a framed autographed photo of *Cheers* star George Wendt. Just try not to yell, "Norm!" when you see it.

CENTRAL WATERS BREWERY

351 Allen St., Amherst, WI 54406; (715) 824-2739; centralwaters.com

Founded: 1996 **Founders:** Mike McElain and Jerome Ebel (with some changes in between). Paul Graham and Anello Mollica have owned it since 2006. **Brewer:** Paul Graham **Flagship beers:** Honey Blonde Ale, Mudpuppy Porter, Quisconsing Red, Satin Solitude Imperial Stout, and Glacial Trail IPA **Seasonal beers:** Summarily American Pale Lager, Octoberfest Lager, and Slainte Scotch Ale **Taproom hours:** Fri, 3 to 10 p.m.; Sat, 12 to 10 p.m.; Sun, 12 to 5 p.m.

You might mistake this brewery for an office park if it weren't for the more than 1,000 feet of solar panels visible from the road (that translates to 120kWh of solar). Managing resources is a big deal to Central Waters Brewery, which sits at the edge of a small farming community. You can't taste renewable energy in the beer, but that kind of commitment shows up in the quality.

Anyone can use reclaimed wood in a taproom, but this taproom sits in lumber country so the barn wood walls and corrugated metal trim make sense. The bar is front and center, but patrons can also get up close to stainless steel tanks full of brew or head to a quiet room away from the bar where they host meetings.

Food trucks visit during the summer. This is Wisconsin, you will see families and children elbowing for a place at the bar. Central Waters serves soda, too, so don't judge.

Central Waters is heralded for its barrel-aged beers. Consider that each year the brewery hosts an anniversary party that inspires thousands to trek to the middle of the state in the dead of winter. The lure is a bottle of anniversary beer available only that day at the brewery and the chance to try others in the Central Water repertoire. It's also the music, the food, and the community. Which is why last year's tickets sold out in under four minutes.

Central Waters makes some of the state's best known and most respected barrel-aged brews. But this is no one-note brewery. People swear by the pale ales and Imperial stouts. The **Honey Blonde Ale** is a cream ale sweetened with a touch of, you guessed it, honey; the **Mudpuppy Porter** has a thick head and a touch of chocolate taste; and the **HHG APA** is an American pale ale whose name was inspired by the music of Horseshoes

BOURBON BARREL SCOTCH ALE

Style: Scotch Ale

ABV: 10 percent

Availability: Special release

Central Waters is known for its aged beers. While some Scotch ales can linger on the sweet side, their **Bourbon Barrel Scotch Ale** is malty and aged until it's smooth. It goes down easily, some might say too easily.

CENTRAL

and Hand Grenades. There's a sense of whimsy to what is arguably great beer. Tap handles are designed as herons.

KOZY YAK BREWERY

197 N. Main St., Roshholt, WI 54473; (715) 677-3082; facebook.com/KozyYakBrewery

Founded: 2012 **Founders:** Rose Richmond and Rich Kosiec **Flagship beers:** Beers change weekly **Taproom hours:** Sat, 3 to 7 p.m.

Co-founders Rose Richmond and Rich Kosiec started out making wine, but a yeast emergency (long story, you should ask) helped Kosiec decide to add beer to their repertoire.

The Kozy part of the name could have been a nod to the location—an old house on the small town's main street. I think I prefer an alternative explanation. Pronounce Richard's last name. Ko-siec. Again. Kozy Yak.

Inside the old house, you can imagine former residents sitting in front of the fireplace or walking up the narrow winding stairs. The stairs are blocked but you can still sneak a peak of the John Travolta poster at the top near the disco ball.

The bar top is fashioned of wine corks and covered in glass. Beer is made behind the French door, which is covered with blue fabric. Little warrens of rooms hold one or two chairs for more intimate conversation.

Kosiec brews on a 2-barrel system and puts out beer in 5-gallon batches, so the beer menu changes frequently. He and Richmond also work full-time jobs, which is why the taproom is open only one day a week. They distribute the beer, but only across town.

When Kozy Yak was open three days a week, Kosiec said they had visitors from all around the state. The farthest anyone came for a beer was Nepal, and he wanted to see what a Wisconsin yak looked like.

MINOCQUA BREWING CO.

238 Lakeshore Dr., Minocqua, WI 54548; (715) 356-2600; minocquabrewingcompany.com

Founded: 2006 **Founders:** Robert Schermetzler, Dan Schermetzler and Walter Houke **Brewer:** Ryan White **Flagship beers:** Whitey's Wheat, Minocqua Pale Ale, Wild Bill's Wild Rice, Road Kill Red, Bear Naked Brown, Pudgy Possum Porter **Seasonal beers:** MBC's Rye IPA and MBC's Hefeweizen **Brewery and restaurant hours:** Tues through Sun, 11 a.m. to 9 p.m. **Upstairs lounge hours:** Wed through Sat, 4:30 p.m. to closing.

This is Northwoods living. Minocqua is on an island in Minocqua Lake and the brewpub and restaurant with the same name overlook the lake. The only distraction from that view is the beer inside. And maybe a sandwich.

Wild rice is a state staple. Adding it to beer is risky business, but brewer Ryan White has the technique down for **Wild Bill's Wild Rice.** The guest ingredient is, as expected, locally sourced and gives the beer a hint of unexpected nutty flavor.

Minocqua Brewing doesn't serve flights, but paddles, a nod to the area's No. 1 draw, which is water recreation. There are spots for seven beer styles, but MBC adds an eighth on the side. One to grow on, perhaps.

The restaurant is on the lower of three levels. Upstairs, patrons can get food at the bar or on the terrace overlooking the shimmer of Lake Minocqua

BEAR NAKED BROWN

Style: Nut Brown Ale

ABV: 6.2 percent

Availability: Year-round

This is how you want to see your bears in Wisconsin—trapped in a glass. Minocqua Brewing's **Bear Naked Brown** is a dark beer with a light, nutty flavor of malts that don't push too hard, just enough to quench a thirst and make you beg for more.

and larger-than-life pine trees. At night, Divans, a lounge, opens for bands, comics and open-mic entertainment.

You'll want to poke around the town, which is surrounded by water. Each autumn, Minocqua hosts Beer-A-Rama, a parade of locals holding roast beef and marching through town. There's an after-parade cook-off and party.

O'SO BREWING

3028 Village Park, Plover, WI 54467; (715) 254-2163; osobrewing.com

Founded: 2007 **Founders:** Marc Buttera and Katina Buttera **Brewers:** It's a team effort. **Flagship beer:** None, really **Tours:** Sat, 2, 3, and 4 p.m. Fee is donated to a charitable cause. **Taproom hours:** Mon through Thurs, 3 to 9 p.m.; Fri and Sat, noon to 10 p.m.

Home brewing is typically the first step to opening a brewery. Not for Marc Buttera. He was home brewing while he and Katina started Point Brew Supply and that's what led to O'so Brewing.

Marc doesn't like to think in terms of flagship beers, but if he had to pick one it might be **The Big O,** a malted wheat beer with a hint of orange that medaled at the 2015 Great American Beer Festival.

O'so Brewing is located in a strip mall anchored on one side by a high-end restaurant and the other by the brew supply store. The brewery in between is visible from the popular taproom. Patrons come in and gather in the middle of the room between the bar and the cozy tables. While we were there, a group was getting a pop on the way to a wedding. Watches

synchronized, they were almost late, but that's what O'so will do. One **Infectious Groove Sour Blonde Ale** is good, another is even better.

Having fun goes hand in hand with the O'so philosophy—the goofy labels, silly beer names, and the tenet written on its packaging: "Brewed by geeks; enjoyed by everyone."

O'so has a growing sour beer program. Barrels are stored in another location—for now. The Butteras purchased twenty acres nearby to build a new facility that will include a brewery but also fruit trees, hops, disc golf, and a campground area.

PIGEON RIVER BREWING COMPANY

1103 N. Main St., Marion, WI 54950; (715) 256-7721; pigeonriverbrewing.com

Founded: 2012 **Founder:** Nate Knaack **Brewer:** Nate Knaack and Brett Hintz **Flagship beer:** Townie Cream Ale, Wet Willy Oatmeal Stout, Buxom Lass Scottish Ale, and Vanilla Jimmy Java Coffee Porter **Seasonal beers:** Scary Larry Pumpkin Ale, Gingerbread Ale, and Bock **Tours:** By request **Taproom hours:** Wed through Sat, 11 a.m. to 10 p.m.; Sun, 11 a.m. to 8 p.m.

In summer of 2016, Pigeon River moved across the street to a bigger facility. It was the result of "Overshooting our goals," said founder Nate Knaack. We should all have these problems. Marion's population of 1,200 supports Pigeon River, but Knaack said some of his regular customers drive an hour or so to enjoy the food and the beer. The move also allowed Pigeon River to carve out a larger kitchen to pump out more hamburgers, pizzas, and wraps.

After your meal, order the **Vanilla Jimmy Java Coffee Porter** with its strong chocolate taste and notes of coffee. Dessert—done and done.

Knaack and Brett Hintz brew together like old friends, which is what they are. The two met in high school where they each played tuba in the band. The conversation and the friendship started with one subject: hops. They still source hops locally, and a little more than a decade later they're still talking about hops.

RED EYE BREWING COMPANY

612 Washington St., Wausau, WI 54403; (715) 843-7334; redeyebrewing.com

Founded: 2008 **Founders:** Kevin Eichelberger, Brett Danke, Pat Cheek, and Dana Wolle **Brewer:** Kevin Eichelberger **Flagship beer:** Thrust! Wisconsin IPA, Man Pants Kolsch, Bloom Belgian Witbier, Scarlet 7 Belgian Dubbel **Seasonal beers:** Oktoberfest **Taproom hours:** Mon through Sat, 11 a.m. to closing

During my visit to Red Eye Brewing, there was a bike club edging its way near my seat at the bar. It was jostling but interesting. They were in no hurry to find a chair, and they had an endless supply of stories, and wallets that opened willingly.

RED EYE THRUST! IPA

Style: American IPA

ABV: 7 percent

Availability: Year-round

Sometimes you just feel bitter. Maybe it's a Friday after a really bad week. Kevin Eichelberger's **Red Eye Thrust! IPA** will transfer those feelings from your heart to your tongue. Move over malts, we've got hops to try.

Founder and brewmaster Kevin Eichelberger rides with a group each week, and his brewing company sponsors a few rides and accepts all kinds—racers, mountain bikes, and snow bikes. Eichelberger said the adventurous are drawn to craft beer. And to Red Eye.

The **Red Eye Quadrupel, Red Eye 2x4,** soothes jostled nerves. The **Afterglow Belgian IPA** goes down smooth after dinner.

Another Wisconsin brewer said she cut her teeth in brewing working as a server at Red Eye. She wasn't old enough to drink, but Wisconsin law let her serve it. Eichelberger told her it didn't matter if she couldn't taste it, she could smell it. And that would give her the information she needed. He didn't know he was setting her up for a successful career as a brewer as well as helping customers get advice from an emerging pro.

ROCKY REEF

1101 1st Ave., Woodruff, WI 54568; (262) 339-1230; rockyreefbrewing.com
Founded: 2015 **Founders:** Christine Forrer and Tyler Smith **Brewer:** Tyler Smith **Flagship beers:** Musky Bite IPA and A Big Red Hen Red Ale **Seasonal beer:** BBC Barrel-aged Amber

Christie Forrer received a degree in marketing and entrepreneurship. She applies it every day at Rocky Reef from the Up North-style tap handles—designed to look like the arrow-shaped signs that identify roads and cabins—to the chalk wall that decodes beer styles.

Forrer and her fiancé Tyler Smith were riding bikes in the vacation community when they saw that the building that is now Rocky Reef was available. Forrer sold her car and the couple moved in with their parents to

save money. After a year, they opened Rocky Reef with a 1-barrel system. Shortly after their first year in business—celebrated with a party—they upgraded to a 10-barrel system. All the better to make more **Up North Lakehouse Saison,** a summer sipper to follow a day on any of the 3,200 lakes in Oneida and neighboring Vilas County.

Beers here are served in 16-ounce Mason jars, which fits the updated country style of the taproom. And those DIY tap handles? They won a first place for branding and design.

Tours of the brewery aren't necessary. Visitors can see beer being made through an oversized window behind the bar.

SAWMILL BREWING CO.

1110 E. 10th St., Merrill, WI 54452; (715) 722-0230; sawmillbrewing.net
Founded: 2016 **Founder:** Stan Janowiak **Brewers:** Richard Irland and Anders Irland **Flagship beer:** They are going to let customers decide **Taproom hours:** Sun through Thurs, 2 to 9 p.m.; Fri and Sat, 2 to 11 p.m.

It took two years of renovation to turn what used to be a Department of Natural Resources building into the Sawmill Brewing Co. It was worth the wait. Inside, the tables are made from trees downed in a 2011 tornado, and it is said there are thirteen species of wood in the flooring. Outside, a patio and fire pit by which to warm your feet await. Sawmill has woods all around; it's like being on vacation.

Sawmill opened with a Kolsch style, an American ale, an IPA, and a brown ale, but the founder and brewers want their customers to decide which will be considered a flagship. In fact, they announce the beers they will be serving daily; it's a big to-do at the brewery. If you want to know and can't make it in person, check out their Twitter or Facebook pages.

Food trucks offer food on weekends and for special events, or you can bring your own in. I might suggest s'mores.

STEVENS POINT BREWERY

2617 Water St., Stevens Point, WI 54481; (715) 344-9310; pointbeer.com
Founded: 1857 **Founders:** George Ruder and Frank Wahle **Brewer:** Gabe Hopkins **Flagship beer:** Dead Blonde Ale **Tours:** Sept through May: Mon through Fri, 1 p.m.; Sat, 11 a.m., 12, 1, 2, 3 p.m.
June through Aug: Mon through Sat, 11 a.m., 12, 1, 2, 3 p.m.; Sun, 12, 1, 2 p.m.

Like Leinenkugel, Miller, and Minhas, Stevens Point is one of the oldest operating breweries in America. Originally founded in 1857, in 2002, brewer Gabe Hopkins came on board and created his **Dead Blonde Ale,** which took first place in an international beer competition in 2016. The brewery also has a limited release series called **Whole Hog** that includes an **Espresso Stout** using coffee from Valentine Coffee Roasters in Milwaukee.

Tours are offered year-round and begin in the gift shop, taking visitors up steps, down steps through the brewery, through packaging, and to the tasting room where they are able to sample a variety of Stevens Point brews not found elsewhere.

An oversized barrel stands in one part of the tasting room with the Point mascot—a tall male figure with a pointy head—that begs for selfies. Tour guides happily talk through the history of the brewery, one that dates back to 1864 when the brewery served beer to the troops in the Civil War.

Another fun fact? Students at the University of Wisconsin at Stevens Point held a Beer Riot in 1967 objecting to a proposed change in the legal drinking age from 18 to 21. The protest drew the attention of Gov. Warren Knowles. The image is part of the University of Wisconsin collection.

TRIBUTE BREWING

1106 N. Bluebird Lane, Eagle River, WI 54521; (715) 480-2337; tributebrewing.com

Founded: 2012 **Founders:** Marc O'Brien and Bill Summers **Brewer:** Marc O'Brien. **Flagship beer:** Twenty-Eight Lake Lager Dortmund, Blueberry Train Wheat, Barefoot Charlie IPA, Ghost Lights Amber Lager Vienna, and Old Eagle Porter **Seasonal beers:** Buckinner Bock, Finn's

Irish Red Ale, White Legs Jalapeño Wheat, Summerwinds IPA, Buck Snort Coffee Stout, and Mele Kalikimaka Coconut Porter **Taproom hours:** Wed through Fri, 3 to 9 p.m.; Sat, 1 to 9 p.m.

On our visit to Tribute Brewing, we see a woman take a seat at the bar and overhear her say that she is having a party and "needs"—her word—bottles of **White Legs Jalapeño Wheat**, a sweet and spicy combination, to serve at said party. But, she explains, she would also like one now. We like her.

The small brewery in an old airplane hangar gets busy when it opens. Residents feel at home here. They helped name the **Old Eagle Chocolate Porter** in a contest, with its typical porter roast taste but also some sour fruits in the body. Vacationers, here for the Cranberry Festival, perhaps, appreciate having a place to go for a growler of fresh beer.

A regular started the collection of sugary Peeps that sit above the bar. Co-founder Bill Summers calls it Tribute's "peeps' show."

The inside of the building is washed in corrugated metal, dark blue paint, and blue lighting, relief from a full day of sun. The town of Eagle River is on a chain of twenty-eight lakes, the largest freshwater chain in the world. In summer, the resort town hosts the Up North Beer Fest. In winter—weather won't stop anyone from visiting—Eagle Rivers hosts the World Championship Snowmobile Derby.

On most days, you'll find Summers behind the bar filling growlers. He collects those from other breweries and his collection numbers 170 and is growing. Patrons are welcome to help themselves to the popcorn offered as a snack or bring in their own food.

GUU'S ON MAIN

1140 Main St., Stevens Point, WI 54481; (715) 344-3200; www.facebook.com/Guus-on-Main-76860951468/?fref=ts
Open Mon through Sat, 11 a.m. to 2:30 a.m.

When you're this close to great breweries you really need to have their beers on tap. Guu's has more than thirty-eight beers, including local brews from Central Waters, Stevens Point, and nearby O'so. The menu isn't bad, either. Burgers are huge and there's a Friday night fish fry. So very Wisconsin.

MILWAUKEE BURGER CO.

2200 Stewart Ave., Wausau, WI 54401; (715) 298-9371; milwaukeeburgercompany.com
Open Sun through Thur, 11 a.m. to 10 p.m.; Fri and Sat, 11 a.m. to midnight

This place might make you forget that burgers and beer are a cliché. Mouth-watering hamburgers can be matched to perfection with a craft beer—especially local ones.

There are locations in Appleton (421 N. Casaloma Drive), Eau Claire (2620 E. Clairemont Ave.), and Pleasant Prairie (9901 77th St.) as well. Hours vary slightly among locations, so be sure to check ahead.

Northwest

Minocqua, Eagle River, and Woodruff are the places people talk about when they talk about "going Up North." It's where you go to drink coffee by the water at sunrise or explore the deep woods of the state.

Yes, Wisconsin has cheese. It's America's dairy land. We make great cheese. Award-winning cheese.

And beer.

Consider that a bonus to getting up close with Wisconsin's camera-ready, adventure-ready geography. There are more than 15,000 lakes in the state and the northwest portion that threads along the mighty Mississippi River is no exception. Here you'll find rolling hillsides, deep woods, and lush green farmland. To the north, the Lake Superior shoreline creates its own beautiful vista.

Get in the car. Don't forget the bike rack. Go.

ANGRY MINNOW

10440 Florida Ave., Hayward, WI 54843; (715) 934-3055; angryminnow.com

Founded: 2004 **Founders:** Jason Rasmussen and Will Rasmussen **Brewer:** Jason Rasmussen **Flagship beers:** Pig American Pale Ale, Charlie's Rye IPA. **Seasonal beer:** 30 seasonal varieties, from Oktoberfest to a summer Hefewiezen. **Tours:** Available upon request **Taproom hours:** Mon, 11 a.m. to 6 p.m.; Tues through Sat, 11 a.m. to 11 p.m.

Lumber was king in this part of Wisconsin. The structure that now houses the Angry Minnow was built in 1890 as the offices of the Northern Wisconsin Lumber Company. Today it's host to events such as the Chequamegon Fat Tire Festival and the American Birkebeiner cross country ski race. Both draw big crowds from the Midwest and beyond. So many that brewer Jason Rasmussen brews a special Belgian ale for the Birdie called **Bitch Hill.**

They also serve up a mean fish fry and smooth ales to locals and vacationers who are drawn by the 858,400-acre Chequamegon National Forest. Or maybe it's the nearby fishing waters. Hayward is home to the Fresh Water Fishing Hall of Fame, which features a 143-foot-long, 41-foot-high Musky out front.

To review: Amazing varieties of beer. Giant musky to visit. Oh, and the area also hosts the Annual Lumberjack World Championships.

BARLEY JOHN'S BREWING

1280 Madison Ave., New Richmond, WI 54017; (715) 246-4677; barleyjohnsbrewery.com

Founded: 2015 **Founders:** Laura Subak and John Moore **Brewers:** Bob McKenzie and J.T. Dalton **Flagship beers:** Wild Brunette Wild Rice Brown Ale, Six Knot IPA, Little Barley Session Ale, and Old 8 Porter **Tours:** You can ask **Taproom hours:** Thurs, 4 to 9 p.m.; Fri, 3 to 10 p.m.; Sat, 1 to 10 p.m.; Sun, 1 to 8 p.m.

John Moore's brewpub in Minnesota outgrew its capacity and, tempted by a couple of business breaks, he crossed the state line to open Barley John's production brewery in New Richmond. Minnesota still gets the good stuff (the taproom remains in New Brighton), but now so does Wisconsin.

To visit, you'll drive through mostly rural rolling countryside before making a turn into what looks like an industrial park. But this industrial park

OLD 8 PORTER

Style: Baltic Porter

ABV: 8 percent

Availability: Year-round

Old 8 Porter from Barley John's pours expectedly dark. It tastes creamy, and you'll find hints of coffee and chocolate that do not overpower. Oh, and smoke. There's the slightest smell of smoke. Great, now I'm thirsty.

has spirit, too. Well, spirits. Parallel 45 Distillery is a bag toss away from Barley John's Brewing.

Look for the big red building to find the brewery. The patio is at the front of the building and there's no doubt that the fire pit gets use on star-powered nights. Windows add natural light inside where the clean design includes an inviting bar but also tables, chairs, and a corner fireplace that is easy to cozy up to on a winter's afternoon.

Taproom manager Kevin Naughton will pour a taste of whatever you desire. Perhaps, the **Mango Pale Ale,** in which the sweetness of the mango is artfully balanced with the citrus of the hops? Or maybe you feel like a **Wild Brunette,** creamy beer spiced by the wild rice and named for Moore's wife. I recommend the porters, though. Tim's **Coffee Hazelnut Porter** has a hint of sweetness. The **Old 8 Porter** is aged in bourbon barrels from next door for eight months and has splashes of vanilla tastes. Wait until both reach room temperature to get the full effect.

Food is served tapas style and a category called "slates" is served just like that, on a slate plate. It's Wisconsin, so of course there's cheese. But the surprise item was the three cranberries dunked in Orangecello and then sugar to soften the tartness. It's good to have a distillery as a neighbor.

Barley John's produced 6,000 to 6,500 barrels during its first year but the sliver of brewery you can view from the taproom is deceptive. It goes back the length of two warehouses. Expansion plans are ahead. Good thing. Barley John's also brews for others.

BLOOMER BREWING COMPANY

1526 Martin Rd., Bloomer, WI 54724; (715) 271-3967; bloomerbrewingco.com
Founded: 2015 **Founders:** Daniel Stolt and Cynthia Stolt **Brewer:** Daniel Stolt **Flagship beers:** Bloomer Beer, Buckingham Ale, and Town Brown **Taproom hours:** Wed and Thurs, 5 to 10 p.m.; Fri, 4 to 10 p.m.; Sat, 1 to 8 p.m.

The building in which Bloomer Brewery is located has a checkered history. Fire destroyed it twice and Prohibition nearly killed it before it saw life as Bloomer Brewery, serving beer to the U.S. Army. However, the end of the war meant the end of Bloomer Brewery.

When it closed, the large stone building was repurposed and chopped into a series of smaller businesses. Daniel Stolt opened his excavating business there in 1985. Things stayed that way until Stolt's home brew hobby grew into a full-time passion. Eventually, Stolt sold the excavating business and brought Bloomer Brewing back to life.

He's since added a 7-barrel system and wants to cask condition lagers in the 35-foot deep well near the bottling system. Stolt brews contemporary beer styles, but he also includes some of the old Bloomer recipes, including **Buckingham Ale,** the most familiar beer to locals who knew the original Bloomer Brewing.

The tasting room is cozy with knotty pine walls and other Up North touches you'll find in the room next door. When the sun flickers through the window just right, it glints off the copper mugs hanging above the bar. These mugs are used by regulars who join the mug club, which includes a free beer on your birthday.

Stepping into the next room will make you swear you are actually in the woods. Mounted heads of prized bucks are fixed to the walls. Stolt doesn't claim them, they belong to the landlord's family of avid hunters.

Visit on a Wednesday to meet the citizens of Bloomer. On a late Saturday afternoon, it's hard to say who you'll find, but the popcorn will flow and the bar will likely buzz with conversation. If you're hungry for more, Firewood Traveling Pizzeria pulls up in the parking lot on Thursdays.

You'll feel like you're getting lost as you drive through the small town of Bloomer, but Stolt thinks history buffs, along with beer lovers, will appreciate the building and its many stories.

BOBTOWN BREWHOUSE AND GRILL

220 W. Main St., Roberts, WI 54023; (715) 749-3979; bobtownbrewhouse.com
Founded: 2015 **Founder:** Mike Christenson **Brewer:** Katie Eells
Flagship beers: Lead Off Runner Cream Ale, Rally Ale Kentucky Common, Without a Doubt Oatmeal Stout, Screamin' Laurie American Blonde Ale, and Lead Off Runner Cream Ale with Cherry **Seasonal beer:** Third Season Pumpkin Porter **Taproom hours:** Mon through Thurs, 10:30 a.m. to midnight; Fri and Sat, 10:30 a.m. to 2 a.m.; Sun, 10:30 a.m. to 11 p.m.

Bobtown is less than two years old, but the list of brews it makes is impressive. The **Lead Off Runner Cream Ale** will taste better with an order of fried cheese curds.

The town of Roberts is a small community not so far from the Minnesota border but just far enough that Twin City residents find it quaint. Founder Mike Christenson was looking for a place to buy when the Bobtown space opened up. He kept the knotty pine walls that are appropriate for the classic small-town Wisconsin bar he wanted to own, but he added a brewery. Christenson and brewer Katie Eells grew up in River Falls, and Christenson said he tried Eells's beer before she ever knew he had tasted it. Then he told her to think about brewing for him, and when he found the spot, Christenson told her: "I'm going to build you a brewery. What do you need?"

"Taplines, for one thing," Eells said. There weren't any when Christenson bought the place, just a cooler of domestic beers, "and New Glarus, of course."

Eells concentrates on beers with clean finishes, no matter which style she is making. There are usually four or five on tap and a specialty beer for Small Batch Thurs, when special releases are offered.

THE BREWING PROJEKT

2000 N. Oxford Ave., Eau Claire, WI 54703; (715) 214-3728; thebrewingprojekt.com
Founded: 2014 **Founder:** William Glass **Brewer:** William Glass **Flagship beers:** WisCoast Pale Ale, GunPowder IPA, and Eauld Alliance Scotch Ale **Seasonal beers:** The Stolen Mile, El DorMino Black IPA, Wisktoberfest, and Jack Eau **Tours:** By appointment **Taproom hours:** Wed and Thurs, 4 to 11 p.m.; Fri, 3 p.m. to midnight; Sat, noon to midnight; Sun, 2 to 8 p.m.

Don't know Eau Claire well? That's why GPS was invented. Don't be worried when you type in the address for The Brewing Projekt and your GPS sends you down residential streets that appear to go nowhere. They go somewhere indeed. Tucked on the edge of a business district, this brewery almost didn't happen. It's a good story; you'll have to talk to founder Will Glass about it on your visit.

You might also ask him about his theory on brewing. In the first year, The Brewing Projekt offered more than fifty beers. "Some are home runs and some are foul balls," Glass said. Some of the home runs include **The Stolen Mile,** an ale brewed with 300 fresh lemons and 10 pounds of fresh basil—you're drooling—and **Jack Eau,** an Imperial bourbon barrel stout with its mouthful of flavors to identify—vanilla, molasses, cinnamon, nutmeg, allspice, and pumpkin.

The brewery's plan is to launch fifty beers every year. You can't hit if you don't swing. Glass is so sure of his theory that he's working on plans for a bigger brewery in the same neighborhood.

Meanwhile, order a pint or a flight from the bar and look around. The brewing equipment is up close and very personal. It's a basic building, but that just makes it homey. In summer, the garage doors are up and open. Picnic tables and strings of lights make the patio a choice spot. Bring your dog.

Besides introducing new beers at a record rate—Glass has some sours in the barrels in the brewhouse—he collaborated with Mikkeller Brewing to create two beers for the 2016 Eaux Claires Festival, a music festival started by native son Justin Vernon. You might know him better as Bon Iver.

BREWSTER BROS. BREWING CO. AND CHIPPEWA RIVER DISTILLERY

406 W. River St., Chippewa Falls, WI 54729; (715) 828-5063; chippewariverdistillery.com

Founded: 2016 **Founders:** Jim Stirn and Kurt Schneider **Brewer:** Jim Stern **Flagship beers:** Rumble Bridge Cream Ale, Wood Tick Pale Ale, Ginger Red Ale, Four Horse India Pale Ale, Dark Timber Stout **Seasonal beers:** Porterville Porter, Tilden Weizen Bier, and Radler (Tilden Wizen with grapefruit juice) **Tours:** Fri, 7 p.m.; Sun, 3 and 8 p.m. **Taproom hours:** Wed and Thurs, 2 to 10 p.m.; Fri and Sat, 2 to midnight; Sun, noon to 6 p.m.

Much smaller than Leinenkugel down the street, Brewster Bros. has a ring-side seat to action on the Chippewa River from a rooftop patio. What was once a video rental store is now a full taproom connected to a distillery, handy on Sunday afternoons when Wisconsinites clamor for their Bloody Marys and a beer chaser.

Tall glass windows show off the copper brewhouse to the public passing by on the main street into town. Long tables designed to mimic those in a German beer hall are scattered throughout, better for customer interaction, the owners say. It works. While we were there, we heard two groups comparing notes on nearby winery and distillery visits.

Inside and out, the renovated storefront is a blend of wood, glass, and corrugated metal. A downstairs patio is bathed in shade while the upstairs version offers unfiltered sun and a nearly 365-degree view of the community. Owner Jim Stern said they've started asking people where they're from and the responses range from a couple blocks away to the West Coast.

Brewster Bros. doesn't serve food, but nearby restaurants are happy to deliver.

DAVE'S BREWFARM

2470 Wilson St., Wilson, WI 54027; (715) 4440-4442; davesbrewfarm.blogspot.com
Founded: 2009 **Founder:** Dave Anderson and Pam Dixon **Brewer:** Dave Anderson **Flagship beers:** Too many to name. **Taproom hours:** Usually open twice a month, Sat and Sun, 3 to 7 p.m. Check the website or Dave's BrewFarm Facebook page to be sure.

A Siebel Institute–trained brewer and Great American Beer Festival judge, Dave Anderson left Minnesota to put down roots on a 35-acre plot of land. He built a wind-generated, sustainable brewery open to the public a couple times a month in this rural city of 184 residents and six taverns. He's easy to find, turn off the highway and it's a straight shot to the BrewFarm.

Groups come with picnic baskets, portable grills, and coolers in all kinds of weather to drink at the bar Dave repurposed from barn wood and an old electrical pole. The BrewFarm also sells Bass Lake Cheese Factory Pizza, in case you didn't bring your own food.

Dave is usually behind the bar just under the vintage light fixture his mother bought for the Anderson family room when he was a kid. Before crowds arrive, Dave pulls out the brewing equipment and brings in long

tables set up like a low-cost wedding reception. A menu of the current beers is tucked behind clear plastic sheets and available at the bar. It's a long list. You'll want to take time to study it.

If you're lucky, **Matacabras,** a name inspired by a Spanish word for wind so strong it can kill goats, is on tap. Matacabras is brewed with rye malts and brown sugar using a Belgian Trappist yeast strain. It's kind of a big deal. Dave is a judge at the Great American Beer Festival, so he knows what good beer should taste like. Other brewers think so, too. Eric Rykal, head brewer at The Brewing Projekt in Eau Claire has been spotted on a busman's holiday trying some of Dave's brews. Who knew brewers giggled so much?

Parking is not an exact science at Dave's, where cars sometimes park each other in or visitors make the hike from the side of the rural road down a small hill to the LaBrewatory, Dave's name for the brewhouse.

No dark taprooms are necessary when you can hang out in bucolic rural Wisconsin sipping brews with a few of your favorite strangers. On a winter's day, I won't lie, it can be a tough drive but it's worth it. Who wouldn't want beer from a guy who named one of his favorite beers after a goat-killing wind? Even if you love goats, it's funny.

LEINENKUGEL

124 E. Elm St., Chippewa Falls, WI 54729; (715) 723-5558; leinie.com

Founded: 1867 **Founders:** Originally Jacob Leinenkugel, now Dick Leinenkugel **Flagship beers:** Honey Weiss, Sunset Wheat, Berry Weiss, Creamy Dark, Leinenkugel's Original, India Pale Lager, and Wisconsin Red Pale Ale **Seasonal beers:** Bigg Butt Doppelbock, Biergarten Tart, Oktoberfest, and a variety of Shandys **Tours:** Every half hour, daily **Taproom hours:** Sun through Wed, 10 a.m. to 6 p.m.; Thurs through Sat, 10 a.m. to 8 p.m.

Either the town grew around Leinenkugel or Leinenkugel swallowed the city whole. The stately brewery, an old barn of a building, and its picturesque campus, is visible through the trees from the parking lot of the Lodge, where everything from tours to afternoon drinking on the patio begins. The Lodge opened in 2003 with a sloping roof that seems out of place without a ski hill behind it. Inside, the four-sided fireplace burns even in summer.

Families and groups walk between enough merchandise displayed—T-shirts, cribbage boards, and, of course, canoe paddles—to resemble a department store, except for the large bar in the corner.

Step up. Drink up. Tours begin every half hour. A guide takes a small group of visitors across a bridge to the brewery complex. It takes at least forty-five minutes to see the whole thing. The original buildings remain

faded, perhaps in homage to the brewery's early beginnings selling beer to the lumberjacks who made their way through the area's logging community.

Now a parcel of SAB Miller (Leinenkugel was purchased by Miller Brewing in 1988), a quarter of Leinenkugel beer is brewed here. Since 1995 Leinenkugel has also been brewed at MillerCoor's 10th Street Brewery in Milwaukee. The sixth generation of Leinenkugel offspring are out marketing the beer and brewery and readying themselves to take over a share of the business, part of the all-in-the-family Leinenkugel history.

But then again, Leinie's considers everyone family. Thousands come to the annual Family Reunion each June for live music, bratwurst, cheese, and beer. It's also a chance for beer fans to meet Jake, Dick, and John, the brothers whose commercials made the beer synonymous with Northwoods Wisconsin.

K POINT BREWERY

4212 Southtown Dr., Eau Claire, WI; (715) 834-1733; facebook.com/kpointbeers

Founded: 2016 **Founders:** Lon Blaser and Tom Breneman **Brewers:** Lon Blaser and Tom Breneman **Flagship beers:** English IPA, Porter, Red Ale, Hefeweizen **Taproom hours:** Wed through Fri, 3 to 10 p.m.; Sat, 11 a.m. to 10 p.m.; Sun, 11 a.m. to 6 p.m.

Lon Blaser and Tom Breneman opened the 7-barrel system in a building adjacent to Coffee Grounds, a shop known for selling fine spirits, beer, wine, cookware, and cooked-to-order foods. The two had been selling their beers from a bar in the center of the store, but expanded in 2016 into the building behind the store. Besides the brewery and taproom, there is seating for sixty and a patio for overflow.

"K Point" is a ski jumping term and is the point of measurement to reach off the jump. K Point calls its beers "blue blazer" because they think they are never out of style. They focus on classic beer styles and brews that would be considered sessional, such as the **Pub Ale,** which has a malty backbone, a dry finish, and a 4.7 percent ABV. For those who like a bigger alcohol content, the **K Point West Coast Ale** with its buttery aroma comes in at 8 percent ABV. Next up, a coffee beer, perhaps?

LAZY MONK BREWING

97 W. Madison St., Eau Claire, WI 54702; (715) 271-0848; lazymonkbrewing.com

Founded: 2010 **Founders:** Leos and Theresa Frank **Brewer:** Leos Frank **Flagship beer:** Bohemian Pilsner, and Bohemian Dark Lager **Seasonal beers:** Rye IPA, Marzin Lager, MaiBock Lager, Oktoberfest, Baltic Porter, Biere De Garde, Helles Pivo, Irish Red Ale, Scottish Ale, and Brown IPA **Taproom hours:** Mon through Thurs, noon to 10 p.m.; Fri and Sat, noon to 11 p.m.; Sun, noon to 10 p.m.

Leos Frank had a corporate job and a home brewing hobby when he decided to open Lazy Monk. "It was his midlife crisis," explains Theresa Frank. "I'm just along for the ride."

Frank knew there was an audience for the style of beers he grew up with, beers made with grains and hops from Germany and the Czech Republic, where Frank is from. The brewery's growth proved him right. He opened Lazy Monk taproom in 2016, marrying the beer house styles to evoke a sense of Europe in the large taproom and outside on the deck. Be sure to pet Lazy Monk's bierhaus dog, Fred, or bring your own.

There are no televisions in the large new space. Strangers share long tables and small baskets of pretzels. Frank wants to encourage conversation

among his clients. Talk about the beer, or talk about the mural on the wall—an Eau Claire artist created it and the couple it depicts represents Leos and Theresa on their wedding day.

Lazy Monk sits on the edge of the Chippewa River where the city is working on creating a bike trail should you want to work off the beer and pretzel calories.

LUCETTE BREWING COMPANY

910 Hudson Rd., Menomonie, WI 54715; (715) 231-6836; lucettebrewing.com
Founded: 2010 **Founders:** Tim Schletty and Michael Wilson **Brewer:** Christian Thompson **Flagship beer:** Farmer's Daughter Blonde Ale **Tours:** By appointment **Taproom hours:** Wed and Thurs, 4 to 10 p.m.; Fri and Sat, 11 a.m. to 10 p.m.; Sun, 11 a.m. to 9 p.m.

Flagship, smagship. "It's all about doing different styles," explains Lucette Brewing co-owner Michael Wilson. "We don't have a traditional seasonal. We do Belgians, a lot of yeast-forward beers like Vienna lager, Bavarians, American, and French."

The story is that Lucette is named for Paul Bunyan's sweetheart. Most everything in this area is named for the tycoons of lumber who helped found the state. For example, Menomonie is home to the University of Wisconsin-Stout, named for lumber baron George Huff Stout. Calling the brewery Lucette was a wink and a nod in that direction.

Although Lucette started life as a production brewery, it's taken a course change in the last two years. There's a new look to the building and, since 2015, the brewery has also served food.

Upstairs, athletic teams gather over long public tables to celebrate a win or drown sorrows over a loss. The centerpieces of the brewery are, yes, the fermenters in the corner but also a Neapolitan pizza oven. Don't let that distract you from making note of the Lucette tap handles, each featuring a different pinup girl, the kind they might have painted on fighter planes during the war.

The restaurant's demographic leans toward local and family. Menomonie is on the small side but it's progressive. So food is locally sourced and often includes gluten-free and vegan options. What you won't find is a television, even in football-crazed Wisconsin. Wilson wanted the brewery to reflect pre-Prohibition breweries where the tavern was the focal point of the community.

"That's what it's turned into," he said. "We've come almost full circle."

When weather allows, a beer garden outside is meant to replicate the many forests in the area with thirty trees and enough wild grasses to make the building look more like a farmhouse and less like the pole shed it once was. It's a good respite for bike riders on the nearby Red Cedar State Trail.

MOONRIDGE BREWING CO.

501 Bridge St., Cornell, WI 54732; (715) 239-1341; facebook.com/MoonRidge-Brew-Pub-1501996800095070/
Founded: 2015 **Founder:** Roger Miller and Cindy Miller **Brewer:** Roger Miller **Flagship beers:** Moonridge Brown Ale and Below the Dam Oatmeal **Tours:** None **Taproom hours:** Mon, 11 a.m. to 10 p.m.; Thurs through Sun, 11 a.m. to 10 p.m.

Roger and Cindy Miller want you to "drink good beer." Roger had been making beer for years when the opportunity to share it with others opened up. MoonRidge has seven beers in the inventory and sells pizza to go with it. But it doesn't stop there. MoonRidge specializes in pizza crust made with the spent grain from brewing and before fermentation so there's no alcohol. The beer marinara sauce, however, is made with, um, beer. Customers fuss over the spent grain crust and offer assistance to those who aren't familiar with it. Recommendations include the **Fisher** honeyweissen brew for a light accompaniment to the Rueben pizza or a **Below the Dam** oatmeal porter to balance the sour of the pizza ingredients.

In a town of 1,300 residents, MoonRidge draws beer lovers from Eau Claire, forty-five minutes away. Business is booming, mostly through word of mouth. Other breweries will send you to MoonRidge and the Millers are happy to return the favor.

NORTHWOODS BREWPUB

50819 West St., Osseo WI 54758; (715) 597-1828; northwoodsbrewpub.com
Founded: 2016 **Founder:** Jerry Bechard **Brewer:** Eddie Rogers **Flagship beers:** Bumb'n Buba's Buzz'n Brew Ale, Floppin' Crappie English Mild **Seasonal beers:** Ripplin' Red Raspberry Wheat, Hefeweizen, Radler, and Habanero porter **Taproom hours:** Mon through Thurs, 11 a.m. to 10 p.m.; Fri and Sat, 11 a.m. to 11 p.m., and Sun, 11 a.m. to 8 p.m.

Travelers on Interstate 94 know the town of Osseo as the home of Norske Nook, a stopping place to get a slice of pie bigger than your head. Not so far away in this town of 4,000 residents is Northwoods Brewpub. It moved from its original home in Eau Claire in 2016 and opened up more

than a place for craft beer and a Friday fish fry. The exterior of the new location looks like an oversized log cabin instead of the former condensery it once was. There's no evidence that evaporated milk was tapped here. Beer is king now.

Inside, it's a hunting lodge for sure. The brewhouse is visible from the bar and you'll spot bright green cans of **Floppin' Crappie,** a beer moniker you're not likely to forget. There are always twenty beers on tap, a couple of them devoted to other Wisconsin brews.

An unusual development deal between Jerry Bechard and Nels Gunderson, a local car dealership owner, allowed for a $2 million upgrade to the century-old building. Upstairs are two floors of reception halls for special events such as weddings or reunions. Grab a pint glass of **Birchwood Pale Ale,** smell the hops, then press a button to take the glass elevators upstairs to ballrooms that are industrial sleek. Or sit outside on the patio (if the weather allows) and watch the ATVs ride in. Northwoods is on the Buffalo River State Trail. However, Bechard isn't done just yet. His plans include opening a distillery in the space on the other side of the brewery.

OLIPHANT BREWING

350 Main St., Suite #2, Somerset, WI 54025; (651) 307-7881; oliphantbrewing.com

Founded: 2014 **Founders:** Matt Wallace and Trevor Wirtanen **Brewer:** Trevor Wirtanen **Beers:** Milk Man Baby Stout, the Gobi and Honeez #2, and others that rotate regularly **Taproom hours:** Thurs, 4 to 9 p.m.; Fri, 4 to 10 p.m.; Sat, noon to 10 p.m.; Sun, noon to 7 p.m.

Friends Matt Wallace and Trevor Wirtanen sharpened their beer making chops at other breweries before opening the tiny but expanding Oliphant Brewing. If it looks a little DIY, it is. The two men did most of the work turning a former 7-Up bottling plant into a brewery on their own. And they're in charge of expansion, which last year meant drywalling a new room and shifting the location of the VHS room, yup, a room where patrons can drink beer and watch movies like *Space Jam.* The barrel club meets there. And by barrel club, they mean you can sponsor one of the brewery's barrel-aged brews. There is always something maturing inside—an English brown ale in a rum barrel for instance. If barrel-aged isn't your thing, try their **Gobias** coffee beer, which sells like hotcakes when the brewery first opens. Others ask for the **Groot,** which uses herbs and spices such as rainbow peppercorns, caraway seeds, cloves, and juniper berries as bettering preservatives instead of hops.

PARTY ON WAYNE

Style: Blonde Ale

ABV: 7 percent

Availability: Year-round

I ordered a sampler on my visit to Oliphant Brewing. The **Party on Wayne** blonde ale stuck out. I don't typically order blonde ales, but then again I don't typically see blonde ales with this degree of alcohol. There's biscuit in my sip. It has a medium body. And that finish is perfectly dry.

Plastic conical fermenters rest in a cooler chilled by three air conditioners to make it the right temperature. Told you, DIY all the way.

Wallace is in charge of production; Wirtanen is the brewer, handling three batches a week on a 3-barrel system. By now, he's brewing double batches five to seven times a week for distribution in Milwaukee, LaCrosse, and Eau Claire. On Sundays, people cross the border from Minnesota to take advantage of Wisconsin's more lax alcohol restrictions.

Wallace admits that the town of Somerset has a party reputation, likely because it's a stop on the Apple River, a nearly 80-mile-long tributary of the St. Croix River and a waterway best known for tubing. Oliphant sells crowlers—32-ounce cans filled with beer and suited to camping and leisurely water sports. Visitors can watch a crowler fill as it happens.

Others come to have a brew in the taproom or on the patio behind the store. Don't let the Suite #2 on the address fool you into thinking Oliphant is in a business park. Rookie mistake. It's at the edge of a little town of rolling hills and village-style stores. If you get lost, stop at the town liquor store, which is owned by Wallace's mother. Oliphant is directly behind it.

PITCHFORK BREWERY

709 Rodeo Dr., Hudson, WI 54016; (715) 245-3675; pitchforkbrewing.com

Founded: 2013 **Founders:** Mike Fredricksen, Jessie Fredricksen, Sarah Edwards, and Jason Edwards **Brewer:** Mike Fredricksen **Flagship beers:** English Porter, Pitchfork Pale Ale, French Toast Ale, Happy Heifer Hefeweizen, SmASH ale, Munich Dunkel, and Sassy's Milk Stout **Tours:** Sun, 2 p.m. (later during Packer season) **Taproom hours:** Wed and Thurs, 3 to 8 p.m.; Fri, 3 to 10 p.m.; Sat, noon to 10 p.m.; Sun, 11:30 a.m. to 7:30 p.m.

This is how friendships should be—You make beer; your friends want to open a brewery. Mike, Jessie, Sarah, and Jason could be the Lucy, Ricky, Fred, and Ethel of brewing but without all the weird antics (though Mike once ran a brewery called 3rd Stall Brewery out of his garage).

The four friends started the brewery together and are now expanding the small-batch nanobrewery into the building next door. Every closet, ever corner, and nearly every bit of space in the rooms behind the bar is dedicated to brewing. They use 100 gallons of ice to chill the beers and try to use ingredients from neighbors when possible. They also like to repurpose what they can, as evidenced by the coasters—they are old CDs.

What isn't recycled is the beer—that's all new! The **French Toast Ale** is served in a glass rimmed with sugar, the **Munich Dunkel** is a smooth drinking malt bomb. Be advised, conversation is difficult to avoid in a place such as this. Not that you want to, it's that kind of bar. Set back in a business park anchored by an Irish pub, Pitchfork attracts those taking a break from the highway and locals who want a refill on a growler. The owners hope to take advantage of two things: The brewery's location close to the Minnesota border where the beer scene is on fire and Wisconsin's more generous Sunday beer laws.

Pitchfork doesn't have a kitchen and food isn't served here, but it's available from Paddy Ryan's Pub just a short walk away. Four other Hudson food spots deliver, and there's fresh popcorn by the basket.

REAL DEAL BREWING

In the Raw Deal organic store; 603 S. Broadway St., Menomonie, WI; (715) 231-3255; facebook.com/RealDealBeer

Founded: 2014 **Founders:** Dan Fedderly and Julie Fedderly **Brewer:** Ryan Verdon **Flagship beer:** Organic Pale Ale **Taproom hours:** The taproom is in the store, which is open Mon through Thurs, 6:30 a.m. to 8 p.m.; Fri and Sat, 6:30 a.m. to 10 p.m.; Sun, 9 a.m. to 6 p.m.

The building that houses the Real Deal nanobrewery might have been an old-fashioned general store in another life with its hardwood floors, high ceilings, and a second story that could easily have held the notions department. Walk in to find smoothies and coffee at one counter, fresh beers at another. One thing guaranteed is that ingredients are all natural. Founders Dan and Julie Fedderly are purveyors of all things raw, vegan, and organic from foods to beverages.

The same goes for brewer Ryan Verdon. Since Real Deal is a nanobrewery, Verdon doesn't need large amounts of hops, which means he can use the freshest hops because they are more readily available in smaller quantities. If he can't get fresh hops, he switches hop style in that beer. If the customer notices, well, that's a cue to have a talk about hops.

Verdon brews eight beers year-round and throws in an experimental beer each year. Be sure to check out the **Organic Pale Ale** with Wisconsin-grown hops and or the **Geoff,** a bold American Strong Ale brewed with un-malted rye from a farm in Minnesota. It tastes hoppy with caramel and spicy rye. Verdon also keeps a gluten-reduced beer or two on tap along with seven guest taps—typically beers that aren't available everywhere. It's kind of a brewer-to-brewer perk. Also be sure to check out the "pour it forward" board. Here's where regulars or strangers can purchase a beer for someone else and leave a note.

Once you've chosen your brew, have a seat in a vintage high-back chair or a table upstairs and enjoy the art show or similar occasion most likely being celebrated.

RUSH RIVER BREWING

990 Antler Court, River Falls, WI 54022; (715) 426-2054; **Founded:** 2004, moved to current site in 2007 **Founders:** Nick Anderson, Dan Chang, and Robert Stair **Brewers:** Anderson and Brett Bakko **Flagship beers:** Bubble Jack IPA, The Unforgiven Amber Ale, Double Bubble Imperial IPA **Seasonal beer:** Nevermore Chocolate Oatmeal Stout, Uberalt Alt Bier, and Kirsch Berlinerweiss **Tours:** 1 p.m. the second Saturday of each month **Taproom hours:** Wed through Fri, 4 to 10 p.m.; Sat, 11:30 a.m. to 10 p.m.; Sun, 11:30 a.m. to 7 p.m.

It would be easy to drive past Rush River, tucked in an industrial park forty minutes from Minneapolis. Heads up: GPS has a little trouble finding it.

It took nine years before Rush River opened up their brewery to a taproom. Better late than never. The beer tastes fresher if you sip while you're sitting in the middle of the brewery where they likely just brewed it. Oh, look. A dog bowl. That one is for Stolli, the brew dog, but on weekends your dog can use it, too.

In summer, a clear sign that you're at the brewery are the people outside at picnic tables. A hiking path invites the curious. Either way, watch the cars cruise in for growler fills.

Co-founder Nick Anderson said Rush River is all about the beer and a constant evolution all the time. They're working on sour brews now and recently added **Uber Alt Bier** to oak barrels for aging. They also make cider for customers who come to the brewery. State law doesn't allow the brewery to sell cider in retail outlets, so this is the only place you'll find it. Another reason to be sure you don't just drive by!

SAND CREEK BREWING

320 Pierce St., Black River Falls, WI 54615; (715) 284-7553; sandcreekbrewing.com

Founded: 1998 **Founders:** Todd Krueger and Jim Wiesender
Brewers: Todd Krueger **Flagship beer:** Oatmeal Stout, Oscars Chocolate Oatmeal Stout, Wild Ride IPA **Tours:** Fri, 3:30 to 6 p.m.
Taproom hours: Thurs, 5 to 10 p.m.; Fri, 3 to 10 p.m.; Sat, noon to 10 p.m.

It's starting to feel like breweries are among the first to embrace repurposing. Sand Creek started out in 1998, but the building that houses it dates back to 1856. It was a brewery then, too, until Prohibition. After that it became a sock company, cold storage for fruits and eggs, and then a turkey farm through the 1960s. Ask co-founder Todd Krueger for a tour and he'll take you to the spot where turkeys once incubated. The building was also used as a creamery and a Coco-Cola bottling plant.

Sand Creek used to be the contract brewer for Furthermore and Cross Plains, but bought the breweries outright in 2016. They still contract brew, having once brewed beers for Half Acre, St. Francis in Wisconsin, and Fall City in Louisville.

Now Sand Creek has eight to ten employees making beer for three breweries. Personally, Krueger likes rich, full-bodied beers. He makes the beers for Griesedieck Bros., a long ago St. Louis beer that was once bigger than Anheuser Busch and that family members hope to bring back. He brews **Lombardi Golden Ale,** a specialty beer from John Lombardi, grandson of beloved Packers coach Vince Lombardi.

Water for the beer comes from the brewery's well. Visitors can take the 1932 elevator down to see the solid walls of the basement and the floor still a little wet from the well.

The taproom here looks like a typical Midwestern basement from the 1960s, except with more beer. The flagships are on tap and maybe a special brew or two.

SOUTH SHORE BREWERY

532 W. Bayfield St., Washburn, WI 54891; southshorebrewery.com

DEEP WATER GRILLE

808 Main St., Ashland, WI 54806; (715) 682-9199
Founded: 1995. **Founder:** Bo Belanger **Brewers:** Bo Belanger and Justin Bohn. **Flagship beers:** Nut Brown Ale, Island Sea Pilsner, Rhoades' Scholar Stout, Northern Lights Cream Ale, and ES Bitter **Seasonal beers:** South Shore Bavarian Wheat, Weizen, Applefest Ale, Porter and Anniversary Ale, E.S.B. Anniversary Ale, and Flanders Red aged in oak **Taproom hours:** Fri, 4 to 8 p.m.; Sat, 2 to 8 p.m.; or whenever the open flag is flying.

When Bo Belanger founded South Shore Brewery, it became the seventh microbrewery licensed in the state of Wisconsin. The brewery was tucked into the center of the Deep Water Grille, which provided both a taproom and a chance to pair the brews with food. The ornate wood bar that looks like it was an original piece to the Deep Water Grille is actually a vintage piece Belanger bought at an auction.

In 2016 Belanger left the bar behind at the Deep Water Grille and set up a brewhouse a few miles away in Washburn. The Tap House, a former bowling alley, offered a larger production area. He added a taproom and the place has become so popular that if he is late to ignite the open sign, people wait outside.

He keeps a turntable moving just behind the bar and the shuffle board game directly in front of the brewhouse windows is made from one of the old bowling alley lanes.

Belanger was a fisheries technician with the Department of Natural Resources before he started South Shore Brewery on the edge of Lake Superior. He sources his base malt from Ashland, and the hops come from nearby farms that he started or helped start. He was among the originators of the Midwest Hops Cooperative, alongside Lakefront, Sprecher, Central Waters, and Bull Falls breweries.

The popularity of his brews and craft beer in general pushed the 2016 expansion to a new location. At the Deep Water Grille, Belanger and his small crew were pulling a double batch of brew each day to keep up with demand, using a conveyor belt from the basement to fill trucks for retail and wholesale accounts and to pump out 1,500 barrels a year.

The small brewhouse remains at Deep Water Grille. Belanger calls it a "nice training ground." But The Tap House is now the main production facility and retail outlet where you can sit at the bar and sip a **Nut Brown Ale** which has a lighter taste than the color indicates or the seasonal **Applefest Ale,** which is homage to the region's apple industry and neighboring Bayfield's Applefest.

SPRING VALLEY GOLF COURSE

345 Hidden Fox Ct, Spring Valley, WI 54767; (715) 778-5513; minescreekbrewing.jimdo.com

Founded: 2014 **Founder:** Guy Leach and Wendy Leach with Dave Boisen and Mines Creek **Flagship beers:** American Cream Ale, South English Nut Brown Ale, American "Dirty" Blonde Ale, and Norwegian Farmhouse Ale **Seasonal beers:** Oktoberfest **Hours:** The clubhouse serves from 11 a.m. to sunset, March to November.

This is the only brewpub on a golf course in the state. So it's worth the meandering trip to get there. And if you make a wrong turn, is it so bad to visit the Crystal Cave, the state's longest cave, beforehand? It's also in Spring Valley. The correct route takes you through a neighborhood of suburban homes and up a hill to the lush greens of the golf course. Head to the clubhouse where the beers inside are super fresh. How fresh? Co-founder Dave Boisen grows the hops.

Samples are offered freely and there are cards on the table with details about the beer styles. **Hooded Cow** cream ale, for instance, is made of 2-row and 6-row barley, roasted malt, and corn combined with two additions of home-grown Mt. Hood hops.

Boisen calls the golf course one of the most scenic in the area. And while there are plenty of seats and televisions to watch inside, there is also an outdoor patio for sipping beer overlooking the 7th hole green.

"We try to follow classic beer styles but with a little twist," Boisen said. The **Dirty Blonde Ale** is darker than a blonde ale is expected to be but true to style. And while they might use juniper berries in the **Norwegian** farmhouse ale, it's because historically, that's how they might have put bitterness into home brews in the era before hops.

THIRSTY PAGAN

1623 Broadway St., Superior, WI 54880; (715) 394-2500; thirstypaganbrewing.com
Founded: 2006 **Founder:** Steve Knauss **Brewer:** Allyson Rolph **Flagship beers:** Northeast Amber Ale, Derailed Ale Pale Ale, Burntwood Black Ale, India Pagan Ale, Lawn Chair Cream Ale, Velo Saison, Trouble Maker Tripel, Yukon, and Mosie **Seasonal beers:** Reinhold Berlin Weisse **Tours:** Sat, 2 p.m. **Taproom hours:** Mon through Wed, 11 a.m. to 10 p.m.; Thurs through Sun, 11 a.m. to 11 p.m.

Technically, Thirsty Pagan is a brewpub, but the pizza and beer share double billing here. Although after two sours, you'll swear the beer wins

YUKON

Style: Mixed Fermentation Sour
ABV: 7 percent
Availability: On tap

I had the Thirsty Pagan's **Yukon** on a hot summer day. It pours a dark red. Sip for a little funk with a hint of raisins and a lick of sour. I still regret not bringing back a growler.

this close race. The building started life as a creamery before becoming a brewery. Now, it's expanded to include a sour program in a warren of rooms in the basement.

The kitchen is on one side in back, the brewery on the other. Brewer Allyson Rolph admits it's a challenge to brew when Thirsty Pagan is busy. Wait staff go in and out a nearby doorway and the flour for the pizza fills the air. But she's handled it.

She compares the small brewing system to her 1992 Toyota pickup—it's paid for and it runs great. There are five small fermenters. She uses a pond pump and a bucket of ice water to recirculate the air. Her specialty brews are the sours she lovingly stores in the basement—most in a room she calls Funky Town, once highlighted by a disco ball. All the sours are named after dogs she knows. She sources ingredients from nature. The yeast in the house saison was collected from a neighbor's plum tree and the rosemary, lemon balm, citrus rind and other botanicals used are from her yard. Be sure to try the **Yukon,** a wood-aged mixed fermentation sour red, or the **Mosie,** a brettanomyoces Brux–finished pale ale.

Local musicians perform in the center room of the restaurant where long tables and more intimate tables get stacked with pizza trays and salad bowls. There are touches of the city here. The 100-year-old bar near the kitchen is left over from the former Tony's Cabaret and the colorful Miller High Life mural across the room is actually a series of panels salvaged from 1951.

If it's nice out, head for the patio where they have six taps running or choose from four firkin pours. These beers aren't available on tap inside; it's a special treat for those taking a seat on the picnic tables. Of course, dogs are welcome.

VALKYRIE BREWING

234 Dallas St., Dallas, WI 54733; (715) 837-1824; valkyriebrewery.com

Founded: 1994 **Founders:** Ann Lee and Randy Lee **Brewers:** Ann Lee and Randy Lee **Flagship beer:** War Hammer Coffee, Oatmeal Milk Porter, Rubee Red Lager, Dragon Blade Lager **Seasonal beers:** Hot Chocolate **Tours:** Sat, 1 p.m. **Taproom hours:** Thurs through Sat, noon to 8 p.m. Hours change seasonally, so be sure to check the website.

In 1995, Ann and Randy Lee built their Viking-themed brewery in a former creamery to become the first microbrewery in Northwest Wisconsin. At one point, the Lees sold the original name—Viking—and changed the brewery's name to Valkyrie, inspired by a female Viking warrior.

Valkyrie doesn't brew many beers straight to style. The Lees like to approach brewing like food with a balance of flavors. Maybe not ones necessarily expected in a beer. For example, their seasonal **Hot Chocolate** is a chocolate oatmeal stout with cocoa and cayenne pepper. Delicious.

The brewery, in a town of 400 residents, considers itself family-oriented. The annual Oktoberfest celebration, which Ann organizes, spreads through town beginning with a pancake breakfast and ending in brats and beer. In between is a Kubb tournament, a Viking lawn game. The event draws 3,000 to 4,000 people.

Time your Valkyrie stop for special occasion nights like Thursdays, which the Lees have tagged "the wurst night." That's when they celebrate brats and beer—you can't get much more Wisconsin. Also visit on art show nights on the first Friday of each month.

CASANOVA LIQUORS

236 Coulee Rd., Hudson, WI 54016; (715) 386-2545; casanovaliquor.com
Open daily, 9 a.m. to 9 p.m.

Operating as the Casanova Beverage Co., until Prohibition, Casanova Liquors is located in a cave that goes 150 feet into the hillside. You can drink beer there during the annual Nova Beer Cave event. Otherwise, feel free to find a seat in front of the fireplace and drink your wine or beer.

THE FIRE HOUSE

202 Gibson St., Eau Claire 54701; (715) 514-0406; facebook.com/theeauclairefirehouse
Open Fri through Sun, 2 p.m. to 2 a.m.; Mon through Thurs, 4 p.m. to 2 a.m.

Chippewa Valley residents voted The Fire House No. 1 for beer selection. Enough said.

THE OXBOW HOTEL AND THE LAKELY

516 Galloway St., Eau Claire, WI 54703; (715) 839-0601; theoxbowhotel.com/restaurant.html
Open Mon through Fri, 7 to 11 a.m. and 5 p.m. to midnight; Sat and Sun, 7 a.m. to 1 p.m. and 5 p.m. to midnight

Late in 2016, Justin Vernon became one of the partners in the boutique Oxbow Hotel. The Lakely is the restaurant inside, the one with all the craft beer. The restaurant's emphasis is on local ingredients and that carries over to the bar. Look for local brews on tap and obviously, live music night.

development to admire the city's modern condominiums.

Not that you should *ignore* the thirteen-time World Champion Green Bay Packers. Lambeau Field glimmers like a gem from the road into town. And when the team plays at home, all the blocks surrounding the stadium take on a Bourbon Street atmosphere, but with cheese curds and beer instead of hurricanes and beignets. Take some time to visit the Packers Hall of Fame along with the Neville Public Museum and the Bay Beach Amusement Park.

On the other side of the bay is Wisconsin's thumb, a slice of picturesque land jetting out into Lake Michigan drawing thousands of tourists each year to enjoy the waterways, resorts, fine dining, and that rare beast, an outdoor theater. Door County pinned its hopes and dreams on cherries and wine but found enough space in recent years to become known for its breweries.

Grab some downtime by riding through Peninsula State Park or take the ferry to Washington Island. You're not that far from civilization. They perform Shakespeare here.

AHNAPEE BREWING

105 Navarino St., Algoma, WI 54201; (920) 785-0822;
Founded: 2013 **Founders:** Brad Schmiling and Aric Schmiling **Brewer:** Nick Calaway **Flagship beers:** Little Soldier Amber Ale and Two Stall Chocolate Milk Stout **Seasonal beers:** Chores Summer Farmhouse Saison, Pumpkin, Oktoberfest, Bavarian Dunkel, and Fun Guy **Taproom hours:** Wed and Thurs, 3 to 9 p.m.; Fri, 10:30 a.m. to 10 p.m.; Sat, noon to 10 p.m.; Sun, noon to 5 p.m.

The town of Algoma is bordered by Lake Michigan on one side. Drivers in a hurry to get to Door County might want to take a beat, grab a beer, and get a pre-taste of relaxation. Now we know that if you're headed to Door County, wine is probably your beverage of choice. Until now, perhaps.

Brothers Brad and Aric Schmiling own Von Stiehl Winery in Algoma. Four years ago they tapped their general manager Nick Calaway to lay the foundation for a brewery. Good thing he has mad brewing skills; there's more at stake than a race against wine. There's history.

Ahnapee was the area's brewery from 1868 to 1886, churning out Ahnapee lager and quenching the thirsts of nearby farmers. Henry Schmiling, a long lost relative of the brothers, was the brewmaster. Today Calaway is making it his mission to stay true to the style he suspects the old brewery produced, sending out brews such as **Gray Wolf,** a Vienna lager he thinks Henry Schmiling might have brewed. He's also keeping his fingers crossed that someone will come to the taproom with a recipe from the historic brewery.

The Great American Beer Festival approved of the brewery's Munich-style Helles and gave the **Long Goodbye** a silver in 2015. Patrons praise it for its light body and honey aroma.

The taproom is tiny, living a former life as a two-car garage. There is just enough room for two people to move behind the bar and seating for maybe twenty around it. If it's nice out, take a seat on the patio overlooking the water and enjoy a glass of **Fun Guy,** a spring brown ale with mushrooms.

You can't tour the brewery but head to the winery next door to see if you can't arrange a look at the basement, which holds barrels of wine. This is where they took advantage of thick walls to lager the beer and tunnels that went under Algoma's streets to distribute it. The tunnels are closed now but you should ask about the ghosts.

The historic brewery's lagering basement does double duty. So do the wine barrels; the seasonal **Helles Red** is aged in red wine barrels.

BADGER STATE BREWING

990 Tony Canadeo Run, Green Bay, WI 54304; (920) 634-5687;
Founded: 2013 **Founders:** Andrew Fabry, Sam Yanda, Mike Servi **Brewer:** Sam Yanda **Flagship beers:** Bunyon Badger Brown Ale, Walloon Belgian Wit Bier, and Green Chop Session IPA **Seasonal beers:** Research and Development specials and more **Tours:** Sat, 4 p.m.; reservations required **Taproom hours:** Wed through Sat, 1 p.m. to close; Sun, noon on non-game days and three hours before kickoff on game days to close

Lambeau Field looms in the near distance. Founders Andrew Fabry, Sam Yanda, and Mike Servi set up a brewery in what was once a locker room for a metal fabrication shop and then grew from there. It might have been a stroke of luck. Mostly, it was the good access to water, electric, and the floor drains that came with the building's former life. Bonus: The rent was cheap because the structure had been vacant for a decade.

The Packer nation tailgates in the area in warmer weather, but they also come in to get a couple beers. There's no restaurant in the taproom so you can bring your own food. In 2015, they opened a dog-friendly patio with corn hole (an outdoor game in which bean bags are tossed into holes for points) and a life-size Jenga game. Last year they opened an event space called the Barrel Haus to host weddings and special events. They also organized a series of special-event concerts at the brewery.

Because they're in the shadow of the stadium or maybe just because the brewery is in Green Bay, Badger State put out **Brett Favre 4ward Pass India Pale Ale** with spices. Expect some of the same from the brewer this year.

On cold Packer game days, there's refuge in nestling on the two leather sofas in a corner of the taproom. Clear window garage doors give a full view of the brewery from the tables scattered throughout. A metal sculpture behind the bar announces that you're at Badger State, complete with a badger paw at the bottom.

COPPER STATE BREWING

313 Dousman St., Green Bay, WI 54303; facebook.com/copperstatebrewing

It's not just Milwaukee. Green Bay is sprouting breweries. But few have a story like Copper State. The owners of Copper State (Jon and Missy Martens, Bill and Emily Heiges, Gregg and Heather Mattek, Brent and Natalie Heliges, Brad and Kristin Heiges, Ben and Andrea Putz, and Ben and Susie Jaeger) purchased its brewery building before the previous tenants were out. A real estate agent heard that Hinterland Brewing planned to move to the new Green Bay Packers Titletown District and negotiated a deal for the building that let Hinterland continue to brew as Copper State simultaneously brewed.

But the Copper State plan doesn't stop at brewing beer. Bill Heiges owns Copper Rock Coffee in Appleton and will brew coffee in the new Copper State.

The coffee shop is on the first floor in an area Hinterland previously used for canning and storage. The building follows the rustic industrial style that Hinterland took advantage of, but features some changes to accommodate a brewery and coffee shop simultaneously. Partner Gregg Mattek said the owners are all related and that visits to Germany helped them decide to concentrate on European-style beers with an emphasis on lagers. Jon Martens is onboard as Copper State's brewer.

DOOR COUNTY BREWING

8099 Hwy. 57, Baileys Harbor, WI 54202; (920) 839-1515; Founded: 2013 **Founders:** John McMahon, Angie McMahon, Danny McMahon, and Ben McMahon **Brewer:** Danny McMahon **Flagship beers:** Little Sister, Pallet Jack Cruiser IPA, Sideshow Belgian IPA, Polka King Porter, and Pastoral Farmhouse Ale **Seasonal beers:** Saison Tropique, Equinox Farmhouse Ale, Ex-Cowboy Nordic Pale Ale, Hank IPA **Tours:** Coming **Taproom hours:** Sun through Thurs, 11 a.m. to 10 p.m.; Fri and Sat, 11 a.m. to 11 p.m. Check the website for seasonal hours.

Look at a map of Wisconsin. See the thumb? That's Door County. That's where Illinois comes to vacation. You're as likely to find a Wisconsin or Michigan license plate here as you are one from Illinois, but you will see a lot of Illinois plates. That's not a bad thing. They get thirsty, too.

The new Door County Brewing will reopen in summer 2017 after three years in another location. This new spot is a bigger facility, necessary for production plans, explained founder John McMahon.

Size might be the biggest difference. There's room for 100 people inside and 60 outside.

Brewer Danny McMahon makes the beers in the Belgian style (he also brews a few of the beers at Octopi Brewing in Waunakee). For example, the **Saison Tropique** blends locally grown Pilsner malt with Munich malt and wheat.

The taproom has a farmhouse theme; they've kept the "feed mill vibe" of the previous place. Think industrial rural. A flannel shirt wouldn't look out

POLKA KING

Style: Porter

ABV: 5.3 percent

Availability: Year-round

You have to order this in Wisconsin. I mean, it's got Polka in the title. The better reason is that it has hints of chocolate thanks to the malt and a little sweetness. Door County Brewing says its named for a tractor-driving Polka master called Freddie Kodanko. So you have to order it for that reason, too.

of place here. And neither does a beard. The men of the McMahon family wear them proudly.

Like the original location—where they've started a sour program—there are no televisions. McMahon remembers one guy stopping him to complain. McMahon told him the idea is to converse and talk to others. At the end of the night, the guy thanked him. He had dinner plans with new friends he had met at Door County Brewing.

FORGOTTEN FIRE BREWERY

N2393 Schact Rd., Marinette, WI 54143; (715) 582-3473; forgottenfirebrewing.com
Founded: 2016 **Founders:** Lindsay Callow and Joe Callow **Brewer:** Joe Callow **Flagship beer:** 5 O'Clock Amber **Seasonal beers:** Cherry Radler **Taproom hours:** Mon through Fri, 10 a.m. to 6 p.m.; Sat and Sun, 10 a.m. to 5 p.m.

Lindsay and Joe Callow opened Forgotten Fire Winery in 2011. Sales were up 30 percent in the summer of 2016, and Joe likes to believe it was the addition of beer tasting. When he says there is something for everyone, he means it. The couple also owns Falling Waters Winery in nearby Crivitz.

The Callows don't brew at the Marinette site, however. They're waiting for licensing on a separate 12,000 square-foot brewhouse next door to the winery. In the meantime, Joe's recipes are made at the Stevens Point Brewery, but sold in the taproom. The flagship **5 O'Clock Amber** was named by friends and employees who would come in on Friday afternoon and raid the owner's beer stock after a week of tasting and drinking wine. The **Cherry Radler** is a German Pilsner blended with cherry soda and doesn't disappoint.

Success in the winery, noting the craft beer trend that drew friends to the winery after hours, and a knowledge of fermentation helped fuel plans for the brewery. Joe says the new brewery will be a production brewery and Wisconsin state law won't allow the Callows to run a restaurant as well. Food will be provided by food trucks or possibly a restaurant group in a nearby building.

HINTERLAND

South Ridge Rd. and Lombardi Ave., Green Bay, WI; (920) 438-8050; hinterlandbeer.com

Founded: 1995 **Founders:** Bill and Michelle Tressler **Brewer:** Joe Karls **Flagship beer:** Packerland Pils and Luna Coffee Stout **Seasonal beers:** Always looking for what's next, what's relevant.

After twenty-one years in the same spot, Hinterland could be considered the grandfather of Green Bay's contemporary craft beer scene. But by the time you read this, the well-respected brewery should be making beer and comfortably passing out plates of food in the new Green Bay Packers' Titletown Entertainment District.

The new spot, an idea sparked during a conversation with Packer executives, is 24,000 square feet with two wood-burning pizza ovens, a wood-burning rotisserie, and two 6-foot-tall wood-burning fireplaces. It's safe to say that owner Bill Tressler loves the idea of a welcoming hearth. The beer magazine reporter turned home brewer turned entrepreneur—he owns Hinterland Gastropub in Milwaukee—is beyond excited about being in passing distance of the hallowed stadium. Hinterland Brewing is one of three anchors for the 34-acre entertainment district just west of Lambeau Field. The district includes a 10-acre family-friendly public plaza. The new space is more than double its former location so expect more production, and more barrel-aged deliciousness like the barrel-aged Belgian quad **Grand Cru** or anything else in Hinterland's **Out of the Woods** series.

HINTERLAND BREWING IPA ON NITRO

Style: American IPA

ABV: 6.7 percent

Availability: Year-round

Hinterland's **IPA on Nitro** pours as creamy as you might expect, and that creaminess brings out some of the malt in a beer more noted for hops. The result is a brew with bright citrus notes but no dry aftertaste.

Watch goings on around you or take the catwalk upstairs to see brewers in action. Diners downstairs are encouraged to share long tables and talk—sports, cheese, sausage, Packers—they're all fair subjects in Wisconsin. Also, beer is an ice-breaker topic. Diners upstairs can interact with chefs while the food is prepared. Tressler thinks the craft beer movement goes hand-in-hand with the local food movement. The food here shines, too.

Garage doors at the back of Hinterland open to the beer garden and the rest of the entertainment district where you can keep an eye on the kids.

LEATHERHEAD BREWING CO.

875 Lombardi Ave., Green Bay, WI 54304; (920) 544-9230; leatherheadbrewingcompany.com
Founded: 2015 **Founders:** Amanda Sharon, Chad Sharon, Jacob Sutrick, Sheila Perks, and Ian Perks **Brewer:** Jacob Sutrick **Flagship beers:** Full Beard Stout, Pritty WITy Witbier, and Boosterseat Farmhouse Ale **Seasonal beers:** Imperial Stout Winter Stout and Blood Orange Witbier **Tours:** You can see the brewery and the process from a table. **Taproom hours:** Sun through Wed, 11 a.m. to 10 p.m.; Thurs through Sat, 11 a.m. to 11 p.m. The hours change on Packer game days.

There were a few surprises in opening a brewpub, according to the Sharons. At first, visitors didn't exactly know how to pour beers at the serve-yourself stations that tappers at selected booths offered. In an area of the taproom called the Beer Wall, customers can choose and pour the size and style of beer they prefer. Instructions are written out, but bartenders are also on hand to help or pour. A few regulars can also help.

The second surprise was the popularity of the **Bearded Stout.** No one doubted that it tasted good, it's an above-average stout full of roasty malts and a hint of sweetness, but they were surprised that it was the best-selling brew of the summer. The expectation was for a lighter beer to take over in this city where winter is the predominant season. And, since it is, they also offer **Imperial Stout Winter Stout** aged in bourbon barrels that once held wine.

Leatherhead is a family business. Amanda Sharon and Sheila Perks are sisters. Brewer Jacob Sutrick is Chad Sharon's cousin. He was the inspiration. Well, his beer was. Sutrick had been brewing in Milwaukee before being lured back home to brew for Leatherhead. Amanda Sharon was a familiar voice on Milwaukee Public Radio before heading back to Green Bay.

Even in the short time they've been around, the Sharons say they have seen the city begin to experiment beyond microbrews to IPAs and sours. They credit their fellow breweries with making good beers to start that trend.

And to encourage them to do the same, the family bought an old crab restaurant located on the same street as Lambeau Field. They renovated the space, and now the only remaining remnants of the crab restaurant are the lighthouse out front and a pub food menu that goes from Greek salads to a hangover burger.

The taproom opens early on Sunday game days and later on Sundays when the game is at night. Check the website to be sure.

RAIL HOUSE RESTAURANT AND BREW PUB

2029 Old Peshtigo Rd., Marinette, WI 54143; (715) 732-4646; railhousebrewpub.com

Founded: 1995 **Founders:** Paul Monnette and Courtney Monnette; Ron Beyer owns it now. **Brewer:** Chris Konyn **Flagship beers:** Silver Cream, Big Mac IPA, and Pilsner **Taproom hours:** Sun through Thurs, 11 a.m. to 10 p.m.; Fri and Sat, 11 a.m. to 11 p.m.

The Rail House Restaurant stands next to the Chicago & North Western railroad tracks. There's history in the brewery. Maybe not this location, but the original had a shady past as a brothel.

The restaurant and taproom are divided. Visitors can see the brewhouse through windows in the taproom. The original back bar is a hand-carved piece of art made in Germany in 1880. You can find an exact reproduction in Las Vegas. Beyer said the crowd is typically local customers, but they get heavy tourists in the summer. And home brewer groups like to host meetings there.

Order a **Silver Cream** or **Brewers' Best Pilsner,** both are based on recipes from the old Menominee-Marinette Brewery, owned by an influential family from nearby Michigan.

STILLMANK BREWING CO.

215 N. Henry St., Green Bay, WI 54302; (920) 785-2337; stillmankbrewing.com

Founded: 2014 **Founders:** Brad Stillmank and Erin Stillmank **Brewer:** Brad Stillmank **Flagship beer:** Wisco Disco, Tailgater Blonde Ale, Perky Porter **Seasonal beers:** Imperial ESB, Maibock, and Oktoberfest **Tours:** Book online. **Taproom hours:** Wed through Fri, 4 to 8 p.m.; Sat, 2 to 8 p.m.

Looking back, co-founder Brad Stillmank understands that maybe his friends loved his college home brews because they were, um, free. But they gave him the confidence he needed to break away from marketing as a course of study and study at the University of California, Davis. He spent a decade working at Ska Brewery in Colorado before coming back to Wisconsin to start his own brewery. Even that didn't happen overnight. Stillmank brewed his beer in Milwaukee while working with a distributor before opening the brewery doors. It paid off. Stillmank is an award-winning brewer these days.

Stillmank the brewery isn't geographically close to Lambeau Field and it's not downtown. It's not close to Titletown or Badger State but they'll direct you to it. You have to look for the former builder's supply warehouse just as the people visiting from Michigan did one day in late summer. Stillmank poured each of them a slim glass of brew, glasses that stand out on a bar that would otherwise be crowded with heavy pint glasses.

There's a view of the brewhouse from every seat in the house. Stillmank has hosted bachelor parties, bachelorette parties, even baby showers. Each Friday after Thanksgiving, he hosts a kegs and eggs event. Look for a special beer to celebrate. Previous choices have included a barrel-age version of the **Perky Porter.**

There is plenty of room for expansion in back, exactly what he has planned. The first year the brewery sent out 325 barrels of brew. In 2016, production reached 1,800 barrels. That's a lot of **Homegrown,** a honey rye ale; **Wisco Disco,** an ESB style ale; and **Perky Porter,** a delicious milk chocolate coffee porter.

TITLETOWN BREWING CO.

200 Dousman St., Green Bay, WI 54303; (920) 437-2337; titletownbrewing.com

Founded: 1996 **Founders:** John Gustavson and Brent Weycker Head **Brewer:** David Oldenburg **Flagship beers:** Boathouse Pilsner, Johnny Blood Red, Dark Helmet Schwartzbier, Green 19 IPA **Seasonal beers:** Bent Tuba Oktoberfest **Tours:** Sun through Tues, 11 a.m. to 9:30 p.m.; Fri and Sat, 11 a.m. to 10:30 p.m. **Taproom hours:** Sun, noon to 9 p.m.; Tues through Thurs, 3 to 11 p.m.; Fri, 3 p.m. to midnight; Sat, noon to midnight

Music floats down from the rooftop patio before you even notice the tower that proclaims this to be Titletown Brewing Co. Take the bridge that crosses the parking lot from the restaurant in the old train depot to the reclaimed 100-year-old vegetable processing factory that houses the brewery, taproom, and the year-round rooftop patio. Of course much of the patio is enclosed. This is Wisconsin. This is Green Bay. You've heard of the Ice Bowl.

Titletown was one of the first craft breweries in town, but it doesn't rest on those laurels. In 2015, the brewery was named large brewpub of the year and brewer David Oldenburg took honors as large brewpub brewer of the year. The crew also brought home a silver for its **Johnny Blood Red** ale in the category of Irish style red ale and for its **SSA** smoke ale. Slowing down? Not a chance.

GREEN 19 IPA

Style: American IPA

ABV: 6.42 percent

Availability: Year-round

Yeah, yeah. I hear you. Another IPA? Trust me, Titletown's **Green 19** is an IPA but not so much that you want a glass of water when you're done.

Titletown's taproom serves twelve to sixteen styles at any one time, which is why they have such a tough time pinning down permanent spots on the list of seasonal beers. Pumpkin? Maybe or maybe not this year. Seasonal styles are brewed at the old brewery across the street where the restaurant is. The brewery taproom is busy enough pumping out everything else. And being available for tours.

Twelve guides with comic timing give the tours—fashioned, they admit, by the similarly memorable tours at Lakefront Brewing in Milwaukee. Keep your eyes open for the water fountain in the basement. We call it a bubbler in Wisconsin. Titletown calls it a Beerbler for obvious reasons. Streams of Johnny Blood Red ale flow from the tap.

A part of the brewery's story is the way it pieced together the old factory and threaded in other artifacts to build the taproom. The cleaned up gear in the front window belonged to the large crane that worked the pressure cookers of the vegetable factory. The foot rail on the bar is from a ride at nearby Bay Beach amusement park. It also set the stage for a soft industrial feel on the rooftop where corrugated metal frames the bar and the smokestacks of the old factory frame the view of the city.

SHIPWRECKED BREW PUB

7791 Wisconsin 42, Egg Harbor, WI 54209; (920) 868-2767; shipwreckedmicrobrew.com

Founded: 1997 **Brewer:** Rich Zielke **Flagship beer:** Summer Wheat, Lighthouse Light Kolsch, Door County Cherry Wheat, and Captain's Copper **Seasonal beers:** Octoberfest **Taproom hours:** Daily, 11 a.m. to 10 p.m.

It's pretty here. Shipwrecked sits on a people-watching stretch of Egg Harbor in Door County where it's all blue skies, Lake Michigan, and acres of cherry trees. The pub was originally built in 1882 as a place for sailors, lumberjacks, travelers, and eventually, Al Capone. The criminal is said to have appreciated the tunnels that run underneath the building.

There are also stories that Shipwrecked is haunted. Maybe the idea is to have a beer to calm your nerves. **Door County Cherry Wheat** takes advantage of the area's most notable product—cherries. Consider the beer your antioxidant of choice then.

Shipwrecked caters to visitors finding respite in the surrounding natural beauty and, of course, the shopping. It builds up a thirst for a pint of **Lighthouse Light** and maybe a game of Cribbage outside on the terrace.

STARBOARD BREWING COMPANY

151 N. 3rd Ave., Sturgeon Bay, WI 54235; (920) 818-1062; starboardbrewing.com
Founded: 2014 **Founders:** Amanda Surfus and Patrick Surfus
Brewer: Patrick Surfus **Flagship beer:** None, strictly intentional
Taproom hours: Wed and Thurs, 3 to 9 p.m.; Fri and Sat, noon to 9 p.m.; Sun, noon to 9 p.m.

Patrick Surfus received a home brewing kit from his mother-in-law. It was the Mr. Beer kit. Patrick used it once. The kit didn't stick, but home brewing did. Amanda and Patrick found themselves heading to breweries on weekends. But it was Ahnapee that convinced Patrick (who convinced Amanda) that brewing on a small system would work commercially.

Patrick says it was "validation or vindication" that you can have a brewery on a small scale. Either way, Sturgeon Bay won.

As the brewer, Patrick won't commit to a flagship beer. "That's kind of our thing," he said. There might be one or two repeats but he's always moving ahead on Starboard's 1-barrel system.

What they wanted was a brewery they would enjoy visiting. And one with food they would like to eat. Technically a brewpub, Starboard serves Door County cheese plates and foods straight from the Mediterranean diet.

Inside the sun shines bright and long tables encourage conversation. You won't find a television inside. The brewery is kid-friendly, too.

BIER ZOT

10677 N. Bay Shore Drive, Sister Bay, WI 54234; (920) 854-5070; facebook.com/BierZot/
Open Wed and Thurs, 3 to 9 p.m.; Fri and Sat, noon to 9 p.m.; Sun, noon to 6 p.m.

Imagine this: You're driving around Door County looking at the scenery and there it is, just past the bowling alley, a beer bar specializing in Belgian beers. It's not a mirage. The gastropub has food to match the decadent list of imported and American craft beers from De Proef and St. Bernardus, to Sixpoint and Salt Lake Brewing Co. The menu also bows to a European influence. These aren't your everyday small plates offerings, plus the view from the patio is waterfront and greenery.

NED KELLY'S PUB

223 Washington St., Green Bay, WI 54302; (920) 433-9306; nedkellyspub.com
Open Mon through Thurs, 3:30 p.m. to 2 a.m.; Fri, 3:30 p.m. to 2:30 a.m.; Sat, 6 p.m. to 2:30 a.m.; Sun, 6 p.m. to 2 a.m.

Beers at Ned Kelly's Pub are arranged by category, beginning with beers $5 and under, then alphabetically from ambers to wheats. There's a section for spice, herb, and vegetable beers. The list of Wisconsin beers draws from the whole state. The menu reflects the entire state.

Multilocation Brewpubs

Corporate brewpubs are making inroads in Wisconsin. If you're from here, it's an indication that you have good taste and want decent beer. If you're not, this might be the taste of home you require.

The Great Dane, Water Street Brewery, and the Milwaukee Ale House are home-grown, multi-location breweries that seem to have found a balance between big menus and small brewhouses.

GRANITE CITY FOOD AND BREWERY

72 West Towne Mall, Madison, WI 53719; (608) 829-0700; gcfb.com/location/madison-wisconsin/
Open Mon through Thurs, 11 a.m. to midnight; Fri and Sat, 11 a.m. to 1 a.m.; Sun, 9 a.m. to 10 p.m.

Granite City was founded in St. Cloud, Minnesota in 1999. Today they have thirty-four restaurants with brewpubs in fourteen states, including one in Wisconsin's state capital. Brewers work with wort sent from the company headquarters.

GREAT DANE PUB AND BREWING CO.

Downtown:123 E. Doty St., Madison; (608) 284-0000
Fitchburg: 2980 Cahill Main, Fitchburg; (608) 442-9000
Hilldale: 357 Price Place, Madison; (608) 320-2772
Eastside: 876 Jupiter Dr., Madison; (608) 442-1333
Wausau: 2305 Sherman St., Wausau; (715) 845-3000
Mon through Thursday, 11 a.m. to 2 a.m.; Fri and Sat, 11 a.m. to 2:30 a.m.; Sun, 10 a.m. to 2 a.m.
greatdanepub.com

Rob Lobriglio is the corporate brewmaster for Great Dane, which opened in 1994 and helped fuel the craft beer movement in Madison and throughout the state. It was the first brewery in the capital city since Fauerbach Brewery closed in 1966.

All but one location brews its own beer. There are eight brews considered flagships, but each Great Dane location has flexibility with what's on tap.

LEGENDS BREWHOUSE AND EATERY

2840 Shawn Ave., Green Bay, WI 54313; (920) 662-1111; legendseatery.com

LEGENDS DE PERE

875 Heritage Rd., De Pere, WI 54115; (920) 336-8036; legendsdepere.com

Legends specializes in ribs and brews such as **Acme Amber, Duck Creek Dunkel,** and **Longtail Light.**

MILWAUKEE ALE HOUSE GRAFTON

1208 13th Ave., Grafton, WI 53024; (262) 375-2337; alehousegrafton.com

The Grafton location, like the downtown Ale House, is also on the Milwaukee River and serves Milwaukee Brewing selections along with guest beers.

ROCK BOTTOM BREWERY

740 N. Plankinton Ave., #1, Milwaukee, WI 53203; (414) 276-3030; rockbottom.com/locations/milwaukee

Dave Bass is the brewer at the Milwaukee location. The brewpub chain, based in Colorado, launched careers of brewers that could fill a hall of fame, if there was such a thing. Rock Bottom sits at the edge of the Milwaukee River so patio diners can watch boats going by or time the bridges when they lift to allow larger boats to pass.

WATER STREET BREWERY

1101 N. Water St., Milwaukee, WI 53202; (414) 272-1195
2615 Washington St., Grafton, WI 53204; (262) 375-1402
3191 Golf Rd., Delafield, WI 53018; (262) 646-7882
140 West Towne Square, Oak Creek, WI 53154; (414) 301-5290

George Bluvas is the brewmaster. The main brewhouse is in Milwaukee. The bright tanks are the first things visitors see at that location. It's the same in Oak Creek where smaller batches are produced. Menu choices range from salads to a sausage platter. Water Street is Milwaukee's oldest brewpub and owner R.C. Schmidt displays an impressive collection of breweriana in each of Water Street Brewery's locations.

MR. BREWS TAPHOUSE

201 S. River Health Way, Appleton, WI 54915; (920) 815-3516
305 W. Johnson St., Madison, WI 53703; (608) 819-6841
610 Junction Rd., Madison, WI 53717; (608) 824-9600
5251 High Crossing Rd., Madison, WI 53718; (608) 422-5424
103 W. Broadway, Suite B, Monona, WI 53716; (608) 286-1131
300 N. Century Ave. Waunakee, WI 53597; (608) 849-4644
611 Hometown Circle, Verona, WI 53593; (608) 845-2280
N91 W15720 Falls Parkway, Menomonee Falls, WI 53051; (262) 415-8138
2012 City Road HH, Plover, WI 54467; (715) 544-4245
All are open Sun-Thurs 11 a.m.-11 p.m. and Fri-Sat 11 a.m. -midnight except the Menomonee Falls location.

This Wisconsin-based craft beer and burger bar started in Weston, Wisconsin, but is branching out to other cities and states with a vengeance.

Annual Events

Wisconsin loves a party. They tailgate in snow and cold on Opening Day. That's what gloves are for—to hold a bottle of beer when your fingers are numb.

Cities such as Kenosha, Green Bay, Madison, and Milwaukee dedicate entire weeks to beer tastings. The state plays host to any number of cultural and music festivals, but when homage is due to brew, we're on it with a festival.

They're all worthy but one draws beer lovers from as far away as Australia. That would be the Great Taste of the Midwest held each August in Madison. Browse the following section to find other events.

JANUARY

CENTRAL WATERS ANNIVERSARY PARTY

Central Waters Brewery, 351 Allen St., Amherst, WI 54406; (715) 824-2739;

Busloads of beer lovers make the trek to central Wisconsin to celebrate in the brewery and, most importantly, take home anniversary brew available only that day and only at the brewery. The payoff for the travel is the chance to listen to live music, grab a brew or two, and then load up with a half dozen bottles of the barrel-aged anniversary brew. Tickets sell out quickly.

ISTHMUS BEER AND CHEESE FESTIVAL

Alliant Energy Center, 1919 Alliant Energy Way, Madison, WI 53713; isthmusbeercheese.com

Beer. Cheese carvings. Beer. Cheese. A cheese and beer school. And beer. The Isthmus Beer and Cheese Festival is one of the busiest festivals of the year. And it's in January when people have to slog through snow to get there.

FEBRUARY

MIDWINTER BREWFEST

Milwaukee Ale House, 233 N. Water St., Milwaukee, WI 53202; (414) 276-2337; http://ale-house.com

Every year on a cold dreary Sunday in February, beer geeks find cheer at the annual Midwinter BrewFest at the Milwaukee Ale House. Hundreds of brews and brewers gather together to raise funds for Midwest Athletes Against Childhood Cancer.

FOND DU LAC BREWFEST

Fond Du Lac County EXPO Building, 561 Martin Ave., Fond Du Lac, WI 54935; facebook.com/FDLBrewfest/

What could be better than a beer festival in the dead of winter? Not much. The festival features more than 200 Wisconsin-only brews.

FOOD & FROTH FEST

Milwaukee Public Museum, 800 W. Wells St., Milwaukee, WI 53233; (414) 278-2728; mpm.edu

Museums are anything but musty. More than seventy breweries pour samples on three floors of the public museum. Wineries and restaurants also have samples to try. And there's live music to enjoy.

MARCH

MADISON ON TAP

Alliant Energy Center, 1919 Alliant Center Way, Madison, WI 53713; (608) 267-3976; alliantenergycenter.com

Last year's festival brought in more than 150 beers for sampling. Enjoy live music while you sip.

HOPS & PROPS

EAA AirVenture Museum, 3000 Poberezny Rd., Oshkosh, WI 54902; (800) 564-6322; eaa.org/en/eaa-museum

Sample beer while you check out the museum's exhibit of vintage airplanes.

ROAR ON THE SHORE

Kewaunee County Fairgrounds, 625 Third St., Luxemburg, WI 54217; kewauneelionsclub.org/brewfest.html

The Lions Club brings in brewers from Wisconsin and Michigan to benefit the charitable and civic improvement activities of the Kewaunee and Dyckesville Lions Club.

APRIL

BETWEEN THE BLUFFS BEER, WINE AND CHEESE FEST

1 Oktoberfest Strasse, LaCrosse, WI 54601; (800) 658-9424; explorelacrosse.com/bluffs-beer-wine-cheese-festival

Celebrate local with more than 200 beers and 45 wines from which to choose. Consider it a spring opener.

CRAFT BREWS AND CHICAGO BLUES FESTIVAL

Geneva National Golf Club, 1221 Geneva National Ave., South, Lake Geneva, WI 53147; (262) 729-4471; brewsandbluesfestival.com

Lake Geneva is home away from home for lots of Chicago residents, so it makes sense that a Lake Geneva beer festival would include Chicago blues. The music is a plus and the setting on a golf course doesn't hurt. But the crown jewel is the chance to sample 100 brews.

CRAFTS & DRAFTS

Serb Hall, 5101 W Oklahoma Ave, Milwaukee, WI 53219; (414) 542-2175; craftsanddrafts.org/home.html

Each year Discount Liquor hosts a day-long beer festival that dovetails with the opening of Milwaukee Beer Week. Sign up for seminars from guest speakers like author Randy Mosher, learn to make beer cocktails, or taste some rare brews. Proceeds go to the Wisconsin Ovarian Cancer Alliance.

DAIRY STATE CHEESE & BEER FESTIVAL

12304 75th St., Kenosha, WI 53142

The Brat Stop—it's a real place—hosts this festival in celebration of Wisconsin cheese and beer from across the country. There's a special event for home brewers.

DELLS RARE BARREL AFFAIR

Mt. Olympus Resort, 1701 Wisconsin Dells Pkwy, Wisconsin Dells, WI 53965; (608) 441-1992

The Wisconsin Brewers Guild celebrates rare and barrel-aged beers, and you're invited. They call it a "springtime celebration of the brewer's art." It's a chance to try the brews that the brewers drink or cellar for themselves.

GITCHE GUMEE BREWFEST

Wessman Arena at the University of Wisconsin, 2701 Catlin Ave., Superior, WI 54880; ggbrewfest.com

You might not have known what Gordon Lightfoot meant when he name-checked Gitche Gumee in his song "The Wreck of the *Edmund Fitzgerald.*" It's the nickname for Lake Superior at the top of the state. The beer festival lets you sample 100 beers from twenty-five different brewers hailing from as far away as Alaska.

STEIN & DINE BEER, CHEESE AND SAUSAGE FESTIVAL

Wisconsin State Fair, 640 S. 84th St., Milwaukee, WI; shepherdexpress.com/steinanddine

Milwaukeeans are often defined by three food groups—beer, cheese, and sausage. Here's a festival that celebrates them simultaneously in one big hall. Includes seminars and, of course, tastings of beer, cheese, and sausage.

KOHLER FESTIVAL OF BEER

The American Club, 419 Highland Dr., Kohler; WI 53044; (920) 457-4441; kohlerathome.com/events-beer.html

Kohler brings together food pairing experiences, tasting soirees, educational seminars, culinary demonstrations, live music, and a 5K Beer Run/Walk. One year this festival included a college kegler-themed party. There are sessions on home brewing, interactive grilling experiences, and chats with brewers and chefs.

MAY

WISCONSIN MICRO-BREWERS BEER FEST

Calumet County Fairgrounds, 900 Francis St., Chilton, WI 53014; (920) 849-2534 rowlandsbrewery.com/beerfest.html

Brewers from all over Wisconsin gather to share some of their popular and rare brews. The fest is hosted by Rowland's Calumet Brewing Co. Bring your own chair to listen to live music.

JUNE

WORLD OF BEER FESTIVAL

Schwabenhoff Pavilion, N56W1450 Silver Spring Dr., Menomonee Falls, WI 53051; wobfest.com

The Beer Barons of Milwaukee, a home brew group, host the annual beer fest, which brings in more than 350 beers, meads, and ciders for tasting. Schwabenhoff provides a selection of German foods and you can expect a polka band or two.

WISCONSIN BEER LOVERS FESTIVAL

Bayshore Town Center, 5800 N. Bayshore Dr., Glendale, WI 53217; (859) 492-9492 or (602) 803-3357; wisconsinbeerloversfest.com

The Wisconsin Brewers Guild hosts the state-centric festival in the middle of a shopping plaza. You sip a beer and shoppers look on jealously.

DOOR COUNTY BEER FESTIVAL

In the park behind the Cornerstone Pub, 8102 School Alley, Bailey's Harbor, WI 54202

If you're going to drink beer on a peninsula, you may as well have a beautiful view. The festival includes beer pairings from chefs, live music, and an array of Wisconsin beers.

GREAT NORTHERN BEER FESTIVAL

Hi-Pines Campground, 1919 UW 45, Eagle River, WI 54521; (800) 359-6315; greatnorthernbeerfestival.com

It's not often you can enjoy brews from more than thirty breweries in a campground in the state's Northwoods. Actually, it's once a year at the Great Northern Beer Festival.

JULY

CHETEK BREW AND RIB FEST

Philips Park, 270 Lakeview Dr., Chetek, WI 54728; chetekbrewfest.com/Welcome.html

Twenty brewers bring samples for you to taste. And then there are the ribs. This July festival typically sells out in April. Better get on it.

MILWAUKEE FIRKIN FEST

Cathedral Square, 520 East Wells, St., Milwaukee, WI 53202; milwaukeefirkin.com

It's fun to say firkin. Brewers from all over the state bring firkins to share at Cathedral Square surrounded by Milwaukee high-rise buildings and live music.

MILWAUKEE BREWFEST

1600 N. Lincoln Memorial Dr., Milwaukee, WI 53202; (414) 321-5000; milwaukeebrewfest.com/welcome.html

Where to look—at the beer in the glass or the vista view of Lake Michigan? I think you can answer that here. Vendors provide food. Brewers provide beer. And there's live music to boot.

LAC DU FLAMBEAU BREWFEST

Torpy Park, Minocqua, WI 54548; (715) 588-3413; acduflambeaubrewfest.com

Live music, a view, and beer. That's how you vacation in one day. Organizers advise fest–goers to ask questions of the many brewers and to thank them. They're so polite.

AUGUST

GREAT TASTE OF THE MIDWEST

Olin Park, 1156 Olin-Turville Court, Madison, WI 53715; greattaste.org

There are two ways to get tickets to the biggest beer festival in the state. Mail in a request to join a lottery or be one of the 200 people who line up late on the first Saturday of the month at various spots in Madison. They share bottles, stories, and often breakfast. It's a prelude to the festival that brings beer geeks together in a park setting. The festival is organized by The Madison Homebrewers and Tasters Guild.

POTOSI BREWFEST

Potosi Brewing, 209 S. Main St., Potosi, WI 53820; (608) 763-4002

More than sixty vendors bring beer, cider, distilled spirits, food, and games to this annual beer festival.

SEPTEMBER

THIRSTY TROLL BREW FEST

Grundahl Park, 2 Parkway Dr., Mount Horeb, WI 53572; (888) 765-5929; facebook.com/events/898443016911818/

The trolls are friendly at this intimate beer festival in small town Mount Horeb. Talk to brewers and sample from twenty-five craft brewers.

ERVTOBERFEST

Erv's Mug, 130 W. Ryan Rd., Oak Creek, WI 53154; (414) 762-5010; ervsmug.com

An annual beer tasting event with a German food buffet. It's small enough that brewery reps bring their rare beers and share them in larger-than-usual portions.

RAILS & ALES BREWFEST

National Railroad Museum, 2285 S. Broadway, Green Bay, WI 54304; facebook.com/events/465701640249437/

If you attended every beer festival in the state you would visit lakes, a campground and events hall. This one is set in a railroad museum. The event includes food, wine, and beer.

GREAT LAKES BREWFEST

Racine Zoological Garden, 200 Goold St., Racine, WI 53402; greatlakesbrewfest.com/main.html

Great Lakes brings brewers from across the country and benefits the Kilties Drum & Bugle Corps in Racine. Oh, to be stranded on Home Brew Island, a big part of the festival.

EGG HARBOR ALE FEST

7809 WI 42, Egg Harbor, WI 54209; (920) 868-3717; eggharboralefest.com

Welcome autumn with a beer in Harbor View Park. More than forty brewers offer samples of 100 beers during the festival. Live music provides the soundtrack.

OCTOBER

MILWAUKEE CIDER & NANO BEER FEST

Schlitz Park, 1543 N. 2nd St., Milwaukee, WI 53212; milwaukeeciderfest.com

Cider rules at this festival, but beer has more than a secondary role. The festival is held on the grounds of the former Schlitz Brewery, you know, the one that made Milwaukee famous.

QUIVEY'S GROVE BEER FEST

6261 Nesbitt Rd., Madison, WI 53719; (608) 273-4900; http://www.quiveysgrove.com

The restaurant pulls out all the stops for its annual beer festival. Nearly fifty brewers pour samples of 100 beers on the restaurant grounds.

NORTHEAST WISCONSIN CRAFT BEER FESTIVAL

Shopko Hall, 1901 S. Oneida St., Ashwaubenon, WI 54304; (800) 895-0071 (tickets), (920) 405-1195 (info); craftbeerfestivalgb.com

Green Bay brewers and those from nearby Algoma, Door County, and Appleton show off their brews and give out unlimited samples to thirsty fest-goers.

DELLS ON TAP

Wisconsin Dells Visitors and Convention Bureau, 701 Superior St., Wisconsin Dells, WI 53965; (800) 223-3557; wisdells.webconnex.com/Dells-On-Tap

Consider this a toast to summer winding down. The Wisconsin Dells is known for its water parks and family fun. The beer festival is a hurrah to a job well done.

BLUE HARBOR CRAFT BEER FESTIVAL

Blue Harbor Resort, 725 Blue Harbor Dr., Sheboygan, WI 53081; (866) 701-2583; blueharborresort.com/craft-beer-festival

The two-day festival includes different levels of tickets with culinary pairings and a chance to try more than 100 craft brews. Package deals for the resort are available.

NOVEMBER

SAVOR MILWAUKEE

Wisconsin Center, 400 W. Wisconsin Ave., Milwaukee, WI 53203; (888) 488-4286; savormilwaukee.com

The event used to be known as Wine and Dine and is produced by the *Milwaukee Journal Sentinel.* Now it's Savor Milwaukee, a wine, beer, and food festival, which gives you a better idea of the current popularity of beer in the food culture. Expect chef demonstrations, beer samples, wine samples, seminars, and cheese island, a land of award-winning cheeses.

Pub Crawls

WALKER'S POINT, MILWAUKEE

As Milwaukee's brewery count grows, your opportunities for fresh suds grow closer together. You can join a private tour of breweries or make your own adventure.

Here's one tour through the Walker's Point neighborhood in Milwaukee (sometimes known as the Fifth Ward).

Start at the **Iron Horse Hotel** (500 W. Florida St.), a former factory turned luxury hotel with a fancy-pants patio called The Yard and a comfortable lobby with deep leather sofas. If you're here on a Thursday, prepare your eyes for the glimmer of chrome. The Iron Horse hosts Harley-Davidson owners for Thursday bike nights any time the weather allows.

Start with breakfast and a Bloody Mary in the hotel's library, or grab a local beer in the lounge called Branded. Branded is known for its craft cocktails, but the beer list is strong with local craft brews, including Fox City Pale Ale from Brenner Brewing. You're headed in that direction. The point is to put down a base.

From here, head directly across the street—you can see it from the hotel's front steps—to:

MobCraft Brewing (505 S. 5th St.). Step up to the long bar inside or find a comfortable chair in back. It might look like the furniture in your parents' basement, but this is vintage folks. And it offers a panoramic view of the brewhouse. The building was abandoned before MobCraft spiffed it up, adding the brewery with enough room for bottling and sour beer aging along with a taproom. The city already had plans to widen the sidewalks on 5th Street, which MobCraft turned into patio space.

What you order here is anything new. MobCraft crowd-sources its beer, which means the public offers up a recipe, MobCraft puts it to a vote, and whichever recipe gets the most pre-orders wins. You'll find new brews and greatest hits in the taproom.

We're walking. We're walking We're walking south. The first thing you'll notice about the street are the many Mexican restaurants. We'll get back to that. But first make your way to:

Brenner Brewing (700 S. 5th St.), where you can get a little culture with your beer. Mike Brenner owned an art gallery before he started his brewery. The labels on each bottle are commissioned artwork. He didn't have to go far to find artists as the brewery is connected to the Pitch Project, a warren of artist studios next door and upstairs from the brewery.

On a warm day, Brenner flings open the garage doors so you barely have to leave the sidewalk to get a beer. If you come late at night, there is a good chance you'll get to see Mike playing accordion (he does play and this is Wisconsin) or catch him singing "Purple Rain" for customers at the end of the night.

Brenner has his own beers on tap here, of course. But he shares space with some of his beer friends from town. One suggestion? Try something he hasn't bottled yet. Be the guinea pig. Someone had to be the first to drink Brenner's wildly successful **Butterfly Farts** farmhouse ale.

From here, we'll be crossing National Avenue, a busy street, so you're going to want to stick together. There's an antique store on one side and shops on the other. We have one more stop for beer on 5th street.

Urban Harvest Brewing (1024 S. 5th St.), where the first thing you'll notice are the vintage windows. Not the big picture windows, although those are nice, but the ones above. They've been here a long time. Owner Steve Pribek scoured those windows before opening the small brewery in 2016. He cleaned them like they were a brew kettle. There's a shiny one of those to the side when you enter. While MobCraft is dark colors and funky décor, and Brenner is open industrial, Urban Harvest has a café style. Small tables dot the room. A wood and glass display case in the corner holds games. Help yourself to fresh popcorn from a machine in the back. There's a chance owner Steve Pribek is behind the bar and a chance that three or four people at the bar live in the neighborhood. They're here for a quick one and a growler fill. Chat them up, along with Pribek. Maybe he'll let you peek in the back room, a full-scale theater with a stage and light booth. There were costumes left behind when Pribek opened in 2016.

Now you have choices. You can retrace your steps back to Brenner and MobCraft or head toward another part of town for fun. You'll want to refuel in any case. If I were making the decisions, I'd head back toward MobCraft to:

Conejito's Place (539 W. Virginia St.), an old-school Mexican restaurant. Take a seat at the counter or share an orange-topped table with strangers. The restaurant has two sides—one dark and tavern-like, the other a little brighter with individual tables. Either way, your food is going to be served on paper plates. I told you, it's old school. One more point: the tortilla chips here aren't free. But they are delicious.

If you've still got the stamina and you know you do, pop across the street to:

Great Lakes Distillery (616 W. Virginia St.) They don't serve beer, but they're in the same sort of family. The folks at Great Lakes were the first in the city to make small batch spirits. If you think about it, visiting breweries and then a distillery is sort of like having a deconstructed boilermaker—a beer followed by a shot.

RIVERWEST, MILWAUKEE

Lakefront Brewery named its Riverwest Stein for the neighborhood where the amber lager was born. Lakefront doesn't brew there any longer, but they remain a big part of the community. The brewery sponsors the morning beer run during the Locust Street Festival of Music and Art each June. A couple other breweries picked up where Lakefront left off. They're in walking distance of each other, which gives you a chance to see the area.

Start at **Fuel Cafe** (818 E. Center St.), from which the coffee used in Lakefront Brewery's Fuel Cafe Coffee Flavored Stout is provided. Sure, go ahead and order one. Black coffee might work better for the adventure ahead but Fuel is not a bad start, either.

Although it's nearby, we're going to save Company Brewing for the end. You'll want a nosh. Keep heading down Center Street to take a look inside

Riverwest Radio (824 E. Center St.), a low-power FM radio station run by the neighborhood's artists, activist, and residents. Alderman Nik Kovac does a show not on politics but on the Green Bay Packers.

If it's after 3 p.m., head north to East Locust Street where you can

pull up a bar stool or a club chair at **Black Husky Brewing** (909 E. Locust St.). You'll likely find owners Tim and Toni Eichinger behind the bar or in the brewhouse. Black Husky tucked itself into Riverwest in 2016, and Riverwest is happy to have them.

When you feel like a change of scenery, head to

Riverwest Public House (815 E. Locust St.). The cooperative pours a decent selection of craft brews at a really good price, part of its mission to "build community one drink at a time."

Hungry? Good. The food matches the quality of the beer at

Company Brewing (735 E. Center St.), where the roasted pork shoulder will set you right up. End the evening with the Night Rye'd Porter on Nitro.

Not ready to call it a night? I have two more suggestions to help you get to know the neighborhood. It's Milwaukee and you seem to have time to spare, so bowling comes to mind. It's a three-minute walk south to Falcon Bowl.

Falcon Bowl (801 E. Clarke St.) offers six lanes of bowling and inexpensive pool, as well as a selection of craft beers on tap. A more ambitious plan would be to go east for a nightcap at **The Gig** (1132 E. Wright St.). That should take about 10 minutes. The small Riverwest pub is often overlooked but it shouldn't be. They've curated a terrific craft beer selection.

GREEN BAY PUB CRAWL

Sure, yes, everyone knows Green Bay for the Green Bay Packers football team. But the city is a rising star among Wisconsin's craft beer producers. Here's a crawl to see some of them.

Start your journey at **Hinterland Brewing** (S. Ridge Rd. and Lombardi Ave.) Hinterland was among the first residents of the Packers' Titletown District, a 34-acre mixed use area with a skating rink, luxury hotel, and Hinterland Brewing. Warm yourself near Hinterland's two 6-foot fireplaces. Grab some food or make a reservation for the chef's table upstairs.

Then hit the road for a ten-minute drive to

Ned Kelly's Pub (223 Washington St.). Ned Kelly's hosts a poker tournament on Wednesday nights. Maybe you'll win enough to take advantage of the cellared beer inventory. If you lose, choose from $5 and under category of beers. They're big on categories here, which makes it helpful when choosing from the menu at "Green Bay's craftiest beer bar."

It's a three-minute drive or a twelve-minute walk to White Dog Black Cat Cafe. You'll want to walk if the weather allows. Head southwest on North Washington Street, take a right onto East Walnut, and then left onto South Broadway and look for the café on the left. Enjoy the walk, you want to be hungry when you get there.

White Dog Black Cat Café (201 S. Broadway St.), where, if it's Friday, you have to go with a fish fry. That's the Wisconsin way and this place serves Walleye, a step beyond the traditional cod. They make it easy by serving lunch, dinner, and breakfast on Sunday.

Head northwest for a short walk to Titletown Brewing and a chance to see the city by foot.

At **Titletown Brewing Co.** (200 Dousman St.) the beer is good and the view is spectacular. Titletown Brewing has a taproom downstairs and a rooftop version a few flights up. Start here and plan your night or just stop for a Johnny Blood Red Irish Ale.

Backtrack south to the Libertine, it gives you a chance to walk past Donald Driver Way. Even if you're not a Packers fan (what?), you'll recall Driver from "Dancing with the Stars."

Libertine (209 N. Washington St.) is known for its craft cocktails. Just looking at the ingredients in the Gunpowder made my mouth water. It's a strategic blend of twelve-year-old Glenfiddich; Cassis Liqueur, Fernet Branca, lemon, cinnamon syrup, and black walnut bitters. Or have a craft beer. The Libertine has twelve taps that rotate weekly, but if that doesn't suit you, they have a list of rare and cellared beers in bottles. This is where your nightcap happens.

Or you could make one more stop for a beer. It's a two-minute drive to

St. Brendan's Inn (234 S. Washington St.) a pub and inn where the beer list is long. Why not grab a Guinness and settle in for some live music?

MADISON 53704 PUB CRAWL

You could shoot a dart at a map of Madison to find a good time. There's one street, though, that guarantees a good time, good beer, and a chance to purchase some vinyl. Atwood Street begins at First Street and ends at Monona Drive and Cottage Grove Road, just enough room to host two summer festivals. You might want to time your visit around the two-day Atwood Fest where they dance in the streets. A Maker Market made its debut at the 2016 festival. The Atwood City Limits Music Festival follows in August.

But for now, start your adventure at the

Sugar Shack Records (2301 Atwood Ave.) sells new and used albums. Name one thing that isn't better with music.

Look across the street. That's the Barrymore Theater (20990 Atwood Ave.), but we're going to double back a step or two to

Next Door Brewing (2439 Atwood Ave.) where there's beer and lots of it. You can see the brewhouse from a seat at the bar or find a table to share and get to know the neighbors. I mean, isn't that the point of Next Door? Quench your thirst or grab an order of cheese curds.

Or save yourself for a burger. Head east to

Harmony Bar and Grill (2201 Atwood Ave.). You can order a salad here, but you're going to want a burger. That's what they do here. Also, they only accept cash. Come back for the live music.

About one minute to the east is

Vault Interiors (2000 Atwood Ave.). Besides the tasteful furniture, they sell cool gifts here. Sometimes retail therapy is just the thing for an adventure.

So is another beer. Directly across the street from Vault is

One Barrel Brewing (2001 Atwood Ave.). Peter Gentry isn't kidding when he says small batches brewed with love. Just behind the bar is the nanobrewery where they pump out love in the form of Commuter Kolsch.

And just because I like the name, I suggest you backtrack west a bit to to hit up

Tex Tubb's Taco Palace (2009 Atwood Ave.) They serve a Frito Burrito, y'all. End the night with a shot of Don Julio 1942 and a side of Wisconsin craft beer. Yes, there are two breweries on this street but Texas Tubb's has brews from Ale Asylum, Lakefront, O'so, Potosi, New Glarus, and St. Francis.

Restaurants with Beer Relationships

A few restaurants in Wisconsin share something with breweries—a name.

RESTAURANTS WITH BEER RELATIONSIPS

MILWAUKEE

ALE ASYLUM RIVERHOUSE

1110 N. Old World 3rd St., Milwaukee 53203; (414) 269-8700; riverhousemke.com

Ale Asylum brews on a lakeside setting? Sign me up. Owner Tim Thompson cut a deal to use the name and serve Ale Asylum beer as the house beer. Ale Asylum Riverhouse isn't otherwise affiliated with the brewery.

JACKSON'S BLUE RIBBON PUB

1203 N. 10th St., Milwaukee 53205; (414) 276-7271; jacksonsbrp.com
11302 W. Bluemound Rd., Wauwatosa 53226; (414) 988-4485

The restaurant has two locations, but to stay in the beer theme, visit the Milwaukee restaurant. It's attached to the Brewhouse Inn and Suites on the Pabst Brewing campus.

POINT BURGER BAR

10950 W. Good Hope Rd., Milwaukee 53224; (414) 797-2970; pointburgerbar.com
W229 N1400 Westwood Drive, Pewaukee, WI 53186; (262) 985-9192

The create-your-own burger bar is a collaboration between Stevens Point Brewery and Milwaukee restauranteur Brian Ward.

SPRECHER RESTAURANT AND PUB

sprecherspub.com

The restaurants aren't owned by Sprecher Brewery but use the name and logo under a licensing agreement with the brewery. The restaurants serve Sprecher beers and sodas. Locations include:

Bayshore Town Center, 5689 N. Bayshore Dr., Milwaukee, WI 53217; (414) 292-0600

111 Center St., Lake Geneva, WI 53147; (262) 248-7047

1262 John Q. Hammons Dr., Madison, WI 53717; (608) 253-9109

644 Wisconsin Dells Pkwy., Wisconsin Dells, WI 53965; (608) 253-9109

820 Indiana Ave., Sheboygan, WI 53081; (920) 451-1500

Beer Gardens

MILWAUKEE

Milwaukee's past is writ in malts and hops. Another piece is garden seating and oversized beer steins enjoyed on a sunny afternoon.

German immigrants found the soil and access to water ideal for brewing beer, and by the 1890s, Milwaukee was the third largest beer producer in the U.S. Along with lager recipes, they brought other traditions like beer gardens. Frederick Pabst commissioned Pabst Park, an 8-acre beer garden with Wild West shows and orchestra performances. Schlitz Park, built in 1879, featured a concert hall, dance pavilion, bowling alley, and a pagoda.

Prohibition, with an assist from electric refrigeration that made beer cellars unnecessary, put an end to the lazy-afternoon beer garden. That was until 2012 when Milwaukee's Estabrook Park hosted the first public beer garden in the country since Prohibition. Hans Weissgerber III, owner of Milwaukee's Old German Beer Hall, brought the idea of reviving beer gardens to the Milwaukee County Parks department, and we couldn't be more thankful.

Don't hate us because we enjoy beer in public gardens near bike paths and walking trails. Join us. Beer gardens are seasonal. They typically open in spring and close in late October. Hours are listed where available.

CROATIAN PARK BEER GARDEN

9100 S. 76th St., Franklin, WI 53132; milwaukeecroatians .org/events/213/croatian-park-beer-garden

Open to the public from 4 to 10 p.m. on specific dates. Check the website.

ESTABROOK PARK BEER GARDEN

4600 N. Eastbrook Drive, Milwaukee, WI 53217; county.milwaukee.gov/Parks/BeerGardens
Open daily at noon. Last call at 9 p.m.

Oompah bands and beer go hand-in-glove at Estabrook. The beer garden is modeled by those in Munich, even down to Hofbrau beer sold. Grab a pretzel, a sausage or on Friday order a fish fry, a Friday night staple in Wisconsin. Be warned: This is a cash only transaction.

Patrons are welcome to bring in food. The park is also open for hiking, disc golf, soccer, and a dog park.

THE LANDING AT HOYT PARK

1800 Swan Blvd, Wauwatosa, WI 53226; friendsofhoytpark.org/Main/The%20Landing/tabid/127/Default.aspx
Open Wed through Fri, 3 to 9 p.m.; Sat and Sun, noon to 9 p.m.

The beer garden is next to the pool run by the Friends of Hoyt Park. A children's playground is steps away. The beer, though, is even closer. The menu is a selection of Wisconsin craft brews along with Miller products. Wine and champagne are also available. Pizza and pretzels are on the menu.

HUMBOLDT PARK BEER GARDEN BY ST. FRANCIS BREWING

3000 S. Howell Ave., Milwaukee, WI 53235; stfrancisbrewery.com/HumboldtBeerGarden.php
Open Mon through Sun noon to 10 p.m.

St. Francis Brewing operates the park, so the brewery's beers are front and center except when the brewery generously opens up for tap takeovers. Breweries from the southern state line to central Wisconsin have participated. There's the occasional pig roast, polka music concert, and trivia night.

TRAVELING BEER GARDENS WITH SPRECHER BREWING CO.

county.milwaukee.gov/parks/beergardens
Open Mon through Fri, 4 to 10 p.m.; Sat and Sun, 11 a.m. to 10 p.m. Last call is 9 p.m.

The Traveling Beer Gardens make fifteen stops during their sixteen-week tours. Sprecher Brewing provides the vehicles—all repurposed emergency vehicles refitted with converted pumps. The trucks set up in picnic areas throughout Milwaukee County Parks and serve Sprecher brews and sodas. Food is available for sale as well.

SOUTH SHORE TERRACE

2900 S. Shore Drive, Milwaukee, WI 53207; http://county.milwaukee.gov/Parks/BeerGardens
Open Wed through Fri, 4 to 10 p.m.; Sat and Sun, 11 a.m. to 10 p.m.

The beer garden sits on the banks of Lake Michigan. Stretch your legs with a waterside walk before sitting down to a beer at the Miller 1855 Bar Area. Gas fire pits warm beer drinkers when the weather won't. The beer garden hosts live music. Nearby are volleyball courts, a boat launch, picnic area, and the Oak Leaf Trail.

HUBBARD PARK BEER GARDEN

3565 N. Morris Blvd, Shorewood, WI 53211, (414) 332-4207; hubbardparkbeergarden.com
Open Mon through Fri, 3 to 10 p.m.; Sat and Sun, noon to 10 p.m.

Privately owned, the nearby Hubbard Park Lodge added a beer garden on its park setting, reviving the beer garden that was there in the 1800s. Hubbard Park Beer Garden sits on a hill above the Milwaukee River and pours a selection of ten beers, including Spaten Lager or New Glarus Spotted Cow.

The garden has picnic tables to share. Bring your own food or share a hot dog or bratwurst bought at the beer stand. Hubbard Park is a stopping point on the Oak Leaf bike trail.

MADISON

Milwaukee isn't the only place in the state to boast beer gardens. Madison has one, too.

MEMORIAL UNION TERRACE

800 Langdon St., Madison, WI; (608) 265-3000; union.wisc.edu/visit/terrace-at-the-memorial-union/

Open Mon through Thurs, 7 a.m. to midnight; Fri, 7 a.m. to 1 a.m.; Sat, 8 a.m. to 1 a.m.; Sun, 8 a.m. to midnight.

Eighty miles to the west of Milwaukee is the most scholarly beer garden of all. The University of Wisconsin in Madison lays claim to the Memorial Union Terrace. Grab a craft beer and take a seat on one of the colorful sunburst chairs that the Union Terrace has become known for. Food is available inside. Live music is often part of the scene. Now take a load off. Relax and look straight ahead at Lake Mendota. See, you're feeling smarter already.

Tours

There's more than one way to see a brewery. Here's a look at brewery tours that get you there by bus, bike, and boat.

HOP HEAD TOURS

Tours breweries in Madison and Milwaukee; (608) 467-5707; hopheadtours.com/milwaukee-bus-tours

Three guys were working at the Great Dane Brewpub when, boom, they got the idea to offer brewery tours. They created Hop Head Tours and now offer a fourteen-passenger bus for tours in Madison and recently added one to Milwaukee.

Take one of these tours and you can expect to learn about the history of brewing in the state and try some beer (they also have distillery and wine tours). Hop Heads has a Beer Titans tour in Milwaukee that begins at the graveyard where four of the barons of brewing are buried. For those who want to work off your beer, Hop Head offers 12-mile bike tours.

Lunch and beer are included in the price. Hop Heads also has special beer tours to Chicago and Michigan breweries.

FUN BEER TOURS MILWAUKEE

Tours Milwaukee breweries with a concentration on the city's beer history; (414) 202-3611; funbeertoursmke.com

Owner Paul Hepp has put together a series of brewery bus tours that not only seek out the city's history in beer, but also plenty of Milwaukee's craft beer bars. Hepp, a collector of breweriana, brings along some of his own prized artifacts to share with the group. Lunch at Jackson's Blue Ribbon and beers are included in the price. Occasionally, so is bowling.

MILWAUKEE FOOD AND CITY TOURS

(414) 255-0534; milwaukeefoodtours.com

Milwaukee Food and City Tours have been giving visitors an inside look at Milwaukee's neighborhoods for more than a decade. They run three beer-related tours: The Pre-Prohibition Historic Bar Tour, the four-hour Craft Breweries & Cocktails Bus Tour, and Bikes, Brats & Beer Tour.

BEST PLACE AT THE HISTORIC PABST BREWERY

901 W. Juneau Ave., Milwaukee, WI 53233; (414) 630-1609; bestplacemilwaukee.com

Brewery tours make it a practice to stop at the Best Place at the Historic Pabst Brewery. But you can go there on your own.

When Pabst closed its doors in the 1990s, things were left behind. Clothing in the lockers, valuable artifacts like old Pabst commercials, and Pabst swag were found during renovation. You can see the former and buy the latter. This is also where you can buy your brewery swag from Schlitz, Old Style, Hamm's, and Old Milwaukee to name a few.

The Historic Pabst Brewery is a step back to a time when this brewery was the big brewery in town. They haven't brewed here since the 1990s; MillerCoors brews Pabst now.

Tours begin in the Steinwert Pub with its vaulted ceilings. The Blue Ribbon Hall has been restored to its original and grand state. Other rooms are decorated in frescos by artist Edgar Miller. Visitors learn the story of how Pabst Blue Ribbon got its name—it isn't what you think. Tours also go upstairs to Captain Frederick Pabst's office. Lovingly restored, the desk is in the spot where Pabst had it, looking over the campus but also with a direct view of where his competitors were in business. You'll hear these stories and maybe get to catch a glimpse of a wedding. Best Place has become a popular spot for ceremonies and receptions.

BREWHOUSE INN AND SUITES

1215 N. 10th St., Milwaukee, WI 53233; (414) 810-3350; brewhousesuites.com

The ninety-room boutique hotel is on the grounds of the former Pabst Brewing complex. The front desk is constructed with 1,500 empty beer bottles. Walk up the stairs to see the sun shine off the tops of the former Pabst copper brew kettles. Ah, yes. Hipster heaven with a chocolate on your pillow.

THE PABST MANSION

2000 W. Wisconsin Ave., Milwaukee, WI 53233; (414) 931-0808; pabstmansion.com

As I write this, the Pabst Mansion is hosting a retro beer night and serving cans of PBR to crowds listening to polka music. They're doing this in an 1892 mansion. The home, which cost $254,000 when it was built, has been restored to its original magnificence.

Captain Pabst added an observatory, which was one the brewery's trade pavilions at the 1893 Colombian Exposition in Chicago. At the center of the pavilion stood a 13-square-foot model of the Pabst Brewing Company's building perched on an elaborate platform supported by gnomes. The structure was built of tan terra cotta and embellished with symbols of the brewing industry including hop vines, beer steins, and the god and goddess of wheat and barley. The pavilion was crowned by a glass art dome. Pabst had the structure dismantled and shipped home from Chicago.

The Pabst is the only mansion spared demolition as the city's population grew and the grand homes of the past were razed in favor of apartment buildings. Tours are offered Monday through Saturday, 10 a.m. to 4 p.m., and Sunday, noon to 4 p.m.

A related look at the Pabst heritage is the Pabst Theater, built in 1895 and designed in the tradition of European opera houses by Otto Strack, the same architect who created the Pabst Mansion.

It wasn't the first iteration of a theater that Pabst had built. The Pabst Theater was a replacement for Das Neue Deutsche Stadt-Theater, which the captain had built in 1890. A fire destroyed it in 1985 and Pabst demanded it be rebuilt at once. The Pabst Theater opened eleven months later.

OLD WORLD WISCONSIN

W372 S9722 Wisconsin 67, Eagle, WI 53119; (262) 594-6301; oldworldwisconsin.wisconsinhistory.org

Old World Wisconsin is an open-air living museum. In 2016, members of the Museum of Beer and Brewing partnered with the museum to brew beer. They used equipment and techniques from the 1800s and heirloom hops and barley grown at Old World Wisconsin. Future plans include a Farmhouse Brewery on the grounds for more public brewing and education.

FOREST HOME CEMETERY

2405 W. Forest Home Ave., Milwaukee, WI 53215; (414) 645-2632; facebook.com/foresthome1850/

Four of Milwaukee's beer barons have their final resting place at Forest Home. The Milwaukee landmark is open to the public. Walk among the graves of Valentin Blatz, Jacob Best, August Krug, and Frederick Pabst.

THE MILWAUKEE COUNTY HISTORICAL SOCIETY

910 N. Old World 3rd St., Milwaukee, WI 53203; (414) 273-8238; milwaukeehistory.net

This museum is in a former brewers' bank building. You can see the vault from the lobby. It holds an extensive collection of history on Milwaukee's brewing history.

THE BEERLINE BIKE TRAIL

traillink.com/trail/beerline-trail.aspx

The Beerline Bike Trail stretches 3.7 miles in Milwaukee with endpoints at West Capitol Drive between North Port Washington Road and North 1st Street to east Pleasant Street and North Commerce Street.

In a former life, freight trains would carry ingredients for beer to the city's famous breweries along this rail. Two disconnected segments of the trail are open: The longer, southern section that runs through the Riverwest, Harambeer, and Brewer's Hill neighborhoods and the second segment that begins at the intersection of Burleigh and Bremen Streets in Riverwest.

BREWERS HILL

historicbrewershill.com

The Milwaukee neighborhood never really had brewers who lived in it. It took its name from its spot overlooking the Schlitz Brewery, which opened in 1870 between Pleasant and Galena, Old World 3rd Street, and the Milwaukee River.

The brewery has been preserved in the Schlitz Office Park, where the Milwaukee Bucks have offices and Manpower has its corporate headquarters. The Brown Bottle, the taproom where the public gathers after a brewery tour, has also reopened here.

On your tour, look around the neighborhood at the historic homes. They sit side-by-side with contemporary homes built to the same measures. Brewers Hill is lauded as one of the city's most integrated neighborhoods. In summer, bring your picnic to Kadish Park where Optimist Theatre presents Shakespeare plays.

Lakefront Brewery moved to the neighborhood in 1998, making it the first brewery on the Beer Line, which borders Brewers Hill.

THE BROWN BOTTLE

221 W. Galena St., Milwaukee 53212; (414) 539-6450; brownbottlemke.com

The Beer Bottle is a museum, but it's also a restaurant, and its located in a renovated building on the Schlitz Brewing campus. If you don't wander the whole campus, at least look at the celebrity pictures on the wall. Dozens of stars visited Schlitz in its heyday, including Lucille Ball. Read the guest book. Imagine the glamour. Bonus: The food is good, too.

WHILE YOU'RE TOURING

Keep your eyes peeled for AJS Tap Handles in the state's many bars and pubs, or even in your own state's bars and pubs. The Wisconsin company designs and manufactures beer tap handles and beer tap markers that sometimes look more like art than industry. They've made more than 500,000 tap handles for brewers from MillerCoors to Mikkeller. Those plastic sheep that suggest you're having a 3 Sheeps beer? They made them. Same with the Central Waters heron and the pointy guy representing Stevens Point.

They've been doing this for more than two decades from a plant in the southern Wisconsin town of Random Lake.

Home Brew Stores

Wisconsinites like to drink beer, but they also enjoy mastering the craft of making it. The businesses in the following section would like to help.

HOME BREW STORES

BREW AND GROW

2246 W. Bluemound Rd., Waukesha, WI 53186; (262) 717-0666 and 1525 Williamson St., Madison 53703; (608) 228-8910; www.brewandgrow.com/retail-locations

BREWMASTERS BREWING SUPPLIES

408 Fond Du Lac Ave., Sheboygan Falls, WI 50385; (920) 467-0441; brewmastersbrewing.com

BULL FALLS BREW DEPOT

606 Washington St., Wausau, WI 54403; (715) 393-4500; bullfallshomebrewdepot.com/page.aspx?index=00000001

FARMHOUSE BREWING SUPPLY

3000 Milton Ave., #109, Janesville, WI 53545; farmhousebrewingsupply.com

HOUSE OF HOMEBREWS

410 Dousman St., Green Bay, WI 54303; (920) 435-1007; houseofhomebrew.com

NORTHERN BREWER

1306 S. 108th St., Milwaukee, WI 53214; (414) 935-4099; northernbrewer.com/about/retail-locations/milwaukee-wisconsin-local-events-and-northern-brewer-classes/

POINT BREW SUPPLY

3038 Village Park Dr., Plover, WI 54467; (715) 342-9535; pointbrewsupply.com

THE PURPLE FOOT

3617 S. 92nd St., Milwaukee, WI 53227; (414) 327-2130; purplefootusa.com

TIKI HUT HOME BREW SUPPLIES

570 Theater Rd., Unalaska, WI 54650; (715) 570-9463; facebook.com/tikihuthomebrew/

U BREW UNIVERSITY

1225 Robruck Dr. A, Oconomowoc, WI 53066; (262) 567-8536

U BREW MILWAUKEE

1101 S 2nd St., Milwaukee, WI 53202; (414) 810-7818; http://ubrewmke.com

Technically, U Brew doesn't sell home brewing equipment or supplies but hosts home brewing classes, workshops, and special events.

WINDRIVER BREWING CO.

861 10th Ave., Barron, WI 54812; (800) 266-4677; windriverbrew.com

WINE AND HOP SHOP

1919 Monroe St., Madison, WI 53711; (608) 257-0099; wineandhop.com

In the Kitchen

I've heard it said that man (and woman) cannot live on beer alone. I don't know if that's true, but I do know something edible made with beer is a good match for a beer tasting or a brewery tour. Here are a few of our favorite recipes that you can make at home. Have fun!

IPA SPINACH ARTICHOKE DIP WITH FRENCH BREAD

From Lakefront Brewery's Kristin Hueneke, Executive Chef

Makes 6 to 8 servings

1 tablespoon olive oil
1/2 cup minced yellow onion
2 (14-ounce) cans chopped artichoke hearts, drained and chopped
1 tablespoon minced garlic
2 pounds fresh spinach, washed and chopped
2 (8-ounce) packages of cream cheese, cut into cubes
11/2 cups sour cream
11/2 cups mayonnaise
2 tablespoons corn starch
2 teaspoons hot sauce
1/2 cup Lakefront Brewery IPA
11/2 teaspoon salt
2 teaspoons ground black pepper
2 teaspoons red pepper flakes
11/2 cups mozzarella
1 cup grated parmesan cheese, plus 1 tablespoon, divided
3 tablespoons melted butter
1 loaf French bread
2 tablespoons minced parsley

Heat olive oil in a medium sauce pan over medium heat. Add onion and sauté until translucent. Keep onions in the pan and add artichokes and garlic. Add spinach one handful at a time until wilted and you can fit it all in the pot. Once all of the spinach has wilted, remove from heat and set aside.

In a large sauce pan combine and heat cubed cream cheese, sour cream, mayonnaise, corn starch, hot sauce, beer, salt, pepper, and red pepper flakes over medium to high heat. Stir occasionally until cream cheese is melted and there are no more chunks.

Slowly add in mozzarella and 1 cup parmesan, stirring continuously. After all the cheese is melted and fully incorporated, add the spinach and artichoke mixture and set aside.

Preheat oven to 400°F.

In a microwave-safe bowl, melt butter for 30 seconds.

Slice French bread into ½-inch slices. Brush both sides with melted butter and place in a single layer on a cookie sheet. Bake for 4 minutes then flip and bake an additional 4 minutes. Remove to serving tray and sprinkle with remaining 1 teaspoon parmesan and minced parsley.

Serve dip warm surrounded by bread slices.

WISCONSIN BELGIAN RED CHOCOLATE SAUCE

From New Glarus Brewing

Makes 6 servings

- 1/2 cup 60 percent cacao dark chocolate chips
- 3 tablespoons heavy cream
- 2 tablespoons cherry all-fruit spread
- 1 tablespoon sugar, optional
- 1/4 cup New Glarus Wisconsin Belgian Red

In a 2-cup microwave-safe container combine chocolate chips, heavy cream, fruit spread, and sugar (if desired). Microwave on high for 40 seconds or until heated through and fruit spread is melted. Stir until well mixed. Add chocolate chips and stir until melted.

Pour in Belgian Red and stir until well blended. Chill for several hours until thickened.

Serve over a piece of your favorite cake or as a dip for fresh strawberries, bananas, or marshmallows.

ALE AND CHEESE SOUP

From Ale Asylum

Makes 6 servings

This is a traditional Wisconsin soup for beer lovers. You can substitute turkey kielbasa to create a healthier version if you choose, with permission from Ale Asylum.

- 1 pound Wisconsin kielbasa, cut into coins
- 1/2 stick butter
- 1 cup diced onion
- 1 cup diced carrot
- 1 cup diced celery
- 2 tablespoon minced garlic
- 2 teaspoon salt
- 2 teaspoon black pepper
- 2 teaspoon ancho chili powder
- 1/2 cup all-purpose flour
- 2 bottles Hopalicious
- 2 cups low-salt chicken broth
- 2 cups cream, divided
- 1 cup whole milk
- 24 ounces shredded Wisconsin cheese (medium cheddar and Monterey Jack work best)
- 1 tablespoon whole fennel, freshly ground
- 1/4 cup minced chives or parsley

Saute kielbasa in saucepan until cooked through, stirring occasionally. Remove, drain, and set aside.

Add butter, onions, carrots, and celery to saucepan over medium heat until they begin to sweat. Add garlic, salt, chili powder, and pepper. Mix well. Whisk in the flour until incorporated with the butter.

Whisk in Hopalicious, followed by the broth and 1 cup of the cream. Bring to a boil, stirring frequently, then reduce to a simmer. Simmer until vegetables are tender, about 10 minutes.

In a separate medium pot, heat remaining 1 cup of cream and whole milk on medium-low until warm. Whisking constantly, add shredded cheese in three batches to the cream until the mixture is completely smooth with no clumps. Add fennel and whisk well.

Add cheese sauce to soup stock and blend until smooth and creamy, (an immersion hand blender works best versus a standard blender). Once blended, simmer soup uncovered for 30 minutes on low heat, stirring occasionally. Add salt and pepper to taste and add the reserved kielbasa. Ladle soup into bowls and garnish with minced chives or parsley.

INDEX